FLORIDA'S GOLDEN GALLEONS

SEARCHING FOR THE TREASURE OF THE 1715 SPANISH PLATE FLEET

By Robert F. Burgess
and Carl J. Clausen

Spyglass Publications

308 W. Marion Street
Chattahoochee, Florida 32324

FLORIDA'S GOLDEN GALLEONS

SEARCHING FOR THE TREASURE OF THE 1715 SPANISH PLATE FLEET

For Julie and Cynthia

Contents

Preface

Our goal was to trace the voyage of a Spanish treasure fleet to its destruction by hurricane on the Florida east coast in 1715, then record the problems and events that occurred 250 years later when the shipwrecks and treasure were found by modern-day treasure hunters. To write the history of such a fleet, we had to know specific details about the circumstances involved. What was it like, for example, to make a transatlantic crossing in the early 18th century? What were the fleet's destinations? Who were the officers involved? What had caused the fateful delays that led to the disaster? How much treasure was lost? What really happened on the night of the hurricane? How did one ship traveling with the fleet escape doom? What was the survivors' fate on the hostile coast far from help?

Hundreds of such questions needed answering, but the pieces of this historical jigsaw puzzle were scattered through the archives of the world. In the search that followed, countless dusty documents, many of which had not been touched since the day they were stored in the archives 250 years before, had to be scrutinized for clues. Official statements, depositions, royal-court orders, private and public letters, ships' manifests, bills of lading — these were the pieces of the puzzle we needed. More than ten years of original research went into the quest for the necessary data. But once these were found, filmed, translated, taped, transcribed and finally filed in a more manageable form of organized chaos, we had the raw material to write the book.

In telling this story we have tried to strike a balance between the dry, unemotional historical facts and a dramatization of the material based on contemporary archaeological information relating to it. We hope the academicians among our readers will forgive us this effort to breathe life into what were assuredly very lively events. For those who might wish to peruse translations of original documents, we have included in the appendices a few of the most important ones consulted during the preparation of the book. Our principal sources of documentary information were: the Museo Naval and the Museo Nacional in Madrid; the Archivos General de Indias, Seville; the Archivo de Simancas, near Valladolid; the British Museum and the Public Record Office, London; the Netherlands Royal Archives in The Hague; the French National Archives, Paris; the Vatican Archives, Rome; the Archivos Generate de la Nacion, Mexico City; the Archives of Jamaica; the National Archives and the Library of Congress, Washington, D.C.; the North Carolina Collection of Spanish Documents in the North Carolina Department of Archives and History; the Stetson Collection of Spanish Documents in the P. K. Younge Library of Florida History, University of Florida, Gainesville, Florida; publications of the St. Augustine Historical Society, St. Augustine, Florida; and numerous books, pamphlets, articles and reference works of the last three centuries. Archaeological material relating to the Spanish fleets was assembled from records of the salvage contract program of the Division of Archives, History and Records Management of the Florida Department of State, from the site records of the Underwater Archaeological Research Section of the Bureau of Historic Sites and Documents, from excavations carried out by the Florida State Museum, and from the original research and publications of both authors.

This work could not have been accomplished without the cooperation and assistance of many colleagues. In appreciation we offer our gratitude to the scientists, scholars, writers, researchers, linguists, librarians, treasure hunters, divers, adventurers and friends who have in some way helped make our task easier. We would especially like to acknowledge the kind assistance of Louis Ullian, a friend and original member of the Real Eight Company; Marjorie Barnes, our always dependable research librarian; and Dr. Eugene Lyon, Professor of History, Indian River Junior College.

Prologue

On July 24, 1715, a Spanish treasure fleet comprised of five ships of the Flota under the command of General Juan Esteban de Ubilla, six vessels of the Galeones fleet commanded by General Don Antonio de Echeverz y Zubiza, and an accompanying French warship, the Grifon, had left Havana, homeward bound for Spain, when they were caught in a hurricane off the Florida east coast near present-day Cape Canaveral. All but the French ship Grifon were wrecked, seven hundred persons perished, and some 14,000,000 pesos' worth of treasure was lost.

To better understand the significance of this event to Spain, one must know something about the history of her treasure fleets, which were largely responsible for Spain's rise to a leading world power.

Their story begins in the late Middle Ages when European nations found they lacked the precious metals necessary to meet the demands of an expanding mercantile trade. It was this quest for new sources of wealth that sent Columbus sailing westward in search of a new route to the riches of the Indies. But instead he found the New World and returned to Spain, where he assured his sovereigns that he had discovered islands containing gold mines.

But in the next twenty years the only wealth that trickled back to Spain was a little gold panned by Indians from the streams of Hispaniola.

After Hernando Cortes conquered the Aztecs (1519-1521), the main flow of wealth was silver from the rich mines of New Spain (Mexico). Then Francisco Pizarro and his conquistadors conquered Peru (1527-1535), and the legendary cities of gold became glittering realities for Spain. In 1545, the Spanish discovered a veritable mountain of silver at Potosi in present-day Bolivia, which produced enormous amounts of the precious metal for Spain for the next fifty years. In addition, the discovery of other rich silver, gold and mercury mines in the New World began to pour an immense wealth into Spain up to the 19th century. Transportation of all these riches back to the Old World was entirely dependent on the success of Spanish treasure fleets.

Each year during the period of the Flota or fleet system in use from the late 16th century to the mid-18th century, two fleets were customarily dispatched from Spain to the New World. One was the Tierra Firma Armada or the Galeones, which collected the trade goods and treasure of South America; the, other was the Nuevo España Armada or Flota, which collected merchandise and treasure accumulated in Mexico. Each fleet consisted of two heavily armed warships — the largest called a Capitana and the other an Almiranta — generally two pataches or patrol vessels, a supply or reinforcement ship, and the merchant vessels or naos sailing under their protection. In wartime, when the treasure fleets were threatened by enemy intervention, the number of protective warships might be increased to eight or twelve, and the merchant ships would travel more heavily armed than usual.

The Flota usually sailed in March and the Galeones in May or June, both fleets following the same general route to the New World. They sailed down the coast of Africa to the Canary Islands, where they left their escorting warships. These would, when practicable, rejoin them in the Azores for the return voyage. Then, with the help of the trade winds and the North Equatorial Current, the ships made their way westward across the Atlantic Ocean. About two months later the fleets sighted Trinidad or the Windward Islands in the West Indies and entered the Caribbean. The Galeones sailed to Cartagena in present-day Colombia to take on the South American treasure. Smaller vessels were dispatched to the island of Margarita to pick up the year's accumulation of pearls from the oyster beds there. Meanwhile, word of the fleet's impending arrival was sent ahead to the governor of Panama so that he could arrange for the Peruvian treasure to be brought north from Lima by other vessels, and then transported across the Isthmus from Panama City to Porto Bello. It was then picked up by the Galeones, which usually returned to Cartagena to winter.

The Flota, which generally arrived in the Caribbean a month or two earlier than the Galeones, proceeded to Vera Cruz, where it took on the treasures and exports of New Spain, along with goods from the Orient that had been brought to Acapulco aboard the annual Manila galleon, then transported overland by mule train to Vera Cruz. Generally, after wintering in this port, the Flota left the following year, catching the prevailing westerly winds on a course that carried the fleet upward into the northern Gulf of Mexico, then southward down the west coast of Florida, passing east of the Dry Tortugas to Havana. There the Flota met the Galeones, which had crossed from Cartagena. Both fleets reprovisioned and then sailed up the Florida Straits, following the Gulf Stream until it veered eastward north of Bermuda, where they caught the prevailing winds that would carry them across the Atlantic to Spain.

Spain's economy was almost totally dependent on these treasure shipments from the New World. Since she manufactured nothing that was needed by other countries, the wealth she received from her New World colonies merely passed through her economy into the economies of other European nations that sold their goods to Spain to fulfill her needs. In a word, other countries benefited more than Spain from her New World wealth. Nearly 95 percent of the precious metals backing European monetary systems came from the Spanish treasure fleets. That is how important they were. When one of these fleets was lost, the whole European economic structure felt the effect. Wars or anything else that interrupted the flow of precious metals from the New World kept the Spanish in debt to international bankers, occasionally with the Crown's customary 20-percent share of the treasure pledged up to five years in advance. Once, when a fleet failed to reach Spain on schedule, Italian bankers threatened to stop all further loans to the Spanish Crown. King Phillip II was so disturbed by this news that he ordered most of the remaining treasure in the royal coffers distributed to various churches and monasteries in Spain for the saying of masses to insure the safe arrival of the fleet. When the ships finally reached Seville, the event was said to have caused great rejoicing throughout the land.

But frequently the fleets failed to reach their destination. The ultimate success or failure of these long voyages depended on the weather. Hurricanes were the worst villains. Throughout the Indies they destroyed more ships, claimed more lives and were responsible for the loss of more treasure than all the pirates or privateers that sailed the seven seas. Between 1525 and 1825, dozens of Spanish treasure ships were lost in Florida waters alone. This is the story of one such fleet.

Chapter 1

Outbound to Oblivion

Standing at the taffrail of his flagship, twenty-seven feet above the water, General Don Antonio de Echeverz y Zubiza, commander of the Galeones, was watching his quartermaster supervise the loading of fruits and vegetables aboard the 700-ton frigate. The commander's fleet of six ships had waited eight months in Havana for the arrival of the Flota, General Don Juan Esteban de Ubilla's four vessels from Vera Cruz. The lengthy wait had been enough to vex a saint, but the fleet from New Spain had had difficulties. No matter how diligently commanders sought to avoid them, General Echeverz would have realized that certain delays were unavoidable. Above all, however, he must have regretted their happening to this particular fleet.

Although Spain customarily sent two annual fleets to collect the treasure of the New World colonies, the recent War of the Spanish Succession (1701-1714) had changed that. The usual sailings of the treasure fleets were curtailed by English and Dutch squadrons in the Atlantic. With the cessation of hostilities in 1712 and the signing of the Treaty of Utrecht, Spain was anxious to reestablish this rich trade with her colonies, particularly the viceroyalties of New Spain and Peru, which had long supplied the lifeblood of her economy—silver. The large amount of merchandise and treasure that had accumulated in the warehouses of the New World during the war was sorely needed in Spain to help defray the cost of that conflict.

The fulfillment of that need rested with the 1715 treasure fleet now assembled in Havana harbor with 14,000,000 pesos worth of treasure and cargo aboard. The combined flotilla numbered twelve ships, including the French warship Grifon, commanded by Captain Antonio Darie. Most of the vessels were low-profile frigates, faster and better designed than the top-heavy galleons formerly used in the Indies trade. Though galleons as a ship type were no longer in use, the romantic term had survived as a name for treasure ships. The fleet's two flagships were large Capitanas, one commanded by General Ubilla, the other by General Echeverz. Next in size and importance were the two Almirantas commanded by admirals. During an attack or any other emergency in which the Capitanas were unable to fulfill their duties, the Almirantas took charge of the fleet. These four warships carried most of the treasure returning to Spain. By virtue of their size and total armament of some two hundred cannon, they would protect the convoy. The remaining vessels were smaller, lighter-armed pataches (tenders), resfuerzos (supply ships) and naos (cargo vessels).

During his long wait for the Flota, General Echeverz knew full well that the later the season, the greater the danger of hurricanes. Sailing late only increased the risk of being caught in the narrow passage between the Bahamas Bank and the Florida reefs by one of those terrible tropical storms. Aware of this fact, the commander became increasingly distressed by the endless delays, particularly since it was now almost August.

This, however, was their final day of waiting, their last delay in loading. The ships would sail with the afternoon tide, and that was a blessing. The general's vessel already looked like a floating garden.

Stalks of bananas and plantains, hampers and sacks of oranges, limes, coconuts and a variety of other fruits and vegetables littered the frigate's main deck. Under the watchful eye of Echeverz's quartermaster, more came aboard on the backs of ragged Indian and Negro stevedores who swarmed alongside the ship in their boats and canoes. Enough water and victuals would be carried to sustain the vessel's five hundred passengers and crew for the almost two-month voyage to Spain. Most of the fresh food would be consumed quickly during the first weeks at sea, as would some of the main stores already laden below — large quantities of hard biscuits, salted meat and fish, dried beef, garbanzo beans, corn, flour, cheeses, oil, vinegar and wine. Pens on the main deck held pigs, chickens, goats, cattle and live sea turtles turned bottoms up. Water was carried in both large and small earthenware jars, wood casks, and six-foot-long sealed segments of bamboo as thick as a man's thigh. Some of these water containers were hung in the rigging; the rest of the supply was stored both above and below decks. For replenishing water stores during the voyage, the frigate carried plaited grass mats which, when leaned along the gunwales from one end of the ship to the other, would catch rainwater and pass it along split bamboo troughs into jars. This process and the dispensing of the vital water ration was in the charge of a seaman called the alguacil de agua, or "water constable." Once the fleet left Havana, it would not stop again to reprovision until it reached Spain.

By 2 P.M. the hot tropical sun beat down mercilessly on the stone and stucco red-tile-roofed buildings and wharves that lined the waterfront. Although it was already the siesta hour, Havana was in no mood to sleep. The departure of the treasure galleons was a day to be celebrated. Colorful flags flew from the somber battlements of El Morro Castle. Their vivid reds, yellows, whites and blacks were repeated in the long pennants and flags waving from the masts and sterns of the massed fleet below. People thronged the narrow cobblestone streets and stone quays at harbor edge. Their voices and guitar music drifted across the water of the bay. Dozens of boats moved back and forth between the quays and the great ships loading the last passengers. Gay crowds of elegantly attired people crossed to the vessels in slender, elaborately carved shallops with up to ten efficient oarsmen. The resplendent colors of the ladies' pastel parasols, broad-brimmed plumed hats and expensive silk dresses made a brave show in the bright sunlight. Not to be outdone, the bewigged gentlemen in their velvet or brocade waistcoats, ruffled shirts and silk pantaloons postured and preened with the nonchalance of peacocks. Less flamboyantly clad soldiers, sailors, servants and other people of lower social standing were transported in smaller, more modest cutters. Baggage for each passenger was supposed to be restricted to two or three trunks or leather-covered chests, a bottlecase or two for wine, and writing materials. Candy, biscuits or anything else could also be carried, so long as it could be kept under the bed. Passengers of some importance often exceeded these restrictions by simple agreement with the captain. The common people carried their belongings in wicker hampers or bags to be kept under their hammocks.

Aboard ship, persons of rank or nobility, frequently royal officials and their families returning to Spain after completing their terms of office in the colonies, were given the choicest accommodations, quite modest by modern standards—quarterdeck cabins the size of small prison cells. Lower-class passengers—men, women and children—shared the same quarters as the crew between decks, where each individual was allotted a tiny six-foot-long space to sling his hammock or lay a pallet, no one more than fourteen inches from his neighbor. The headroom in these quarters was usually five feet four inches or less. On General Echeverz's Capitana, the largest ship in the fleet, the gun deck was 160 feet long and less than 45 feet wide. More than 450 persons were relegated to this cramped, dark, damp space. At sea, when all hatches and ports would often be closed, sometimes for weeks, the air below decks would become foul enough to extinguish a candle.

Every cubic inch of space not occupied by a passenger

was crammed with cargo or baggage. When the hold, cabins and companionways were filled, bales and chests were piled along the main decks, despite a law of 1608 that confined all cargo to the hold. Spanish treasure ships were frequently overloaded. Often cannon were detrunked and stored below along the keel in rows, muzzle to cascabel, to lower the ship's center of gravity and thus permit more cargo to be carried above. General Ubilla's flotilla was no exception.

Finally, the last passenger was aboard and the last official formality performed. The ships were ready, the men standing by. Spectators and passengers waited calmly, expectantly. Havana's cathedral bells signaled the last ritual. General Echeverz gazed across the harbor to the sea, but what he was really looking at was the sky. Nothing marred the flawless pale blue rim except a single wispy mare's-tail cloud on the northern horizon. Then he saw Ubilla's flagship hoist the signal to make sail. The commander of the Galeones murmured an invocation, turned brusquely away from the rail and gave the order.

A cannon aboard the flagship of the Flota boomed hollowly, relaying the signal to the more distant ships of the fleet. Officers bellowed orders, and bare feet pounded the decks as crews sprang into action. Men scurried up the ratlines and out the yards. Headsails blossomed from forestays and rose rippling and flapping, the breeze blowing down both sides. Clouds of canvas billowed aloft, while sweating men heaved the creaking capstan bars around to the rhythmic clanking of the capstan pawls. Slowly the thick hemp cables came home, water oozing out of the fiber strands and running down the decks. Seamen at the bows shouted when the massive oak anchor stocks hove into sight, streaming mud and silt from the harbor bottom.

On General Echeverz's Capitana, men at the sheets hauled the yards round until flapping canvas caught the breeze and boomed full foresails and mains. Slowly, ponderously, the great ship moved forward under reduced sail, gradually gaining speed, a "bone in her teeth" as she pushed a small hillock of water ahead of her stubby bows. On shore the crowds cheered and shouted farewells.

One by one the ships lumbered into line behind their respective flagships. The awakening of the massed armada was a spectacle long to be remembered as the Plot a led the way: General Ubilla's 471-ton, 50-gun Capitana, Nuestra Señora de la Regia, followed by his three tenders and supply vessels; then the 315-ton, 40-gun French warship, the Grifon, and finally, the Rota's 450-ton, 54-gun Almiranta.

Then came the Galeones fleet: General Echeverz's 713-ton, 72-gun Capitana, Nuestra Señora del Carmen, leading his smaller patache and resfuerzo, then the two prize vessels captured earlier off South America — the small frigate La Francesa and the sloop La Galera. The last warship in line was the fleet's 312-ton, 40-gun Almiranta.

In majestic splendor the ships moved toward the sea, ghosting across the water like swans, the heavily armed men-of-war with their gunports raised to expose their tiers of menacing cannon.

High above the harbor a rumbling tattoo of drums rolled from the ramparts of El Morro Castle, where a black-robed archbishop blessed the fleet while impassive officials, bedecked in gold braid, hoped fervently that this flotilla of vessels, with its huge treasure so sorely needed by the Empire, would safely reach Spain.

Twelve times the fortress's cannon roared their measured salutes, and twelve times they were answered by the departing fleet.

The twelve vessels under sail were an impressive sight as they swung out of the harbor with their crested flags flying, their decks crowded with people waving a last farewell.

Once the ships were clear of the headland, crews scurried aloft to break out all sails. Topsails and gallants shook free and filled with a bang. The ships gained speed, heeling heavily into the coastal currents. From that moment on, the long-awaited Spanish treasure fleet of 1715 was set on a course destined for a rendezvous with modern history.

Chapter 2

The Gathering Storm

As treasure ships had done since the mid-16th century, the 1715 fleet would follow the New Bahamas Channel, the straits between Florida and the Bahamas Islands. But rather than go by the short, direct route north into the unknown reefs and labyrinthine Florida Keys, or even northeast up the safe deepwater axis of the Straits, it chose a longer, more devious route. The reason was simple. Navigation was still a hit-or-miss proposition. There were few straight lines in the sea lanes when ships were at the mercy of winds and currents, so there was much beating back and forth in the ocean to get anywhere. Since no one could be certain exactly where he was, once out of sight of land, Spanish pilots in charge of the fleet's navigation felt safer sailing for known landmarks or hazards so that they could see and avoid them, rather than confronting the unknown in the open ocean. Therefore, vessels taking the longer and supposedly safer way to reach the relatively narrow passage between Florida and the Bahamas steered a course that kept the fleet close to land. As soon as the ships left Havana harbor, then, they swung east along the coast of Cuba, traveling only as fast as their slowest vessel. With favorable winds and currents, the armada averaged almost six nautical miles an hour.

Twelve hours out of Havana, the lookouts sighted Punto Ycaco, a prominent point overgrown with coconut palms. For vessels following the eastern route to the Straits, this was their last view of Cuba as the ships altered course to the east-northeast for Cayo Sal, a small group of islands thirteen leagues away where the Spaniards often made salt. Prior to leaving Havana, the fleet's officers had been soundly briefed on all the bearings, course changes and landfalls from Havana through the Straits to the point where the ships veered eastward across the Atlantic to Spain. For obvious reasons it was vital for the fleet to travel together and for everyone to understand the route that lay ahead. From Cayo Sal the course was northwest five leagues to Muertos Cayos (Deadman's Keys), more than a hundred great rocks the size of vessels that thrust up out of the ocean on the west end of the Double-Headed-Shot Keys; then north-northeast twenty-three leagues to Los Membros (Riding Rocks), barren rocks that look like wrecks. At this point the fleet would sail west-southwest across the Florida Straits for nineteen leagues until it approached the Cape Reef in latitude 25°2'N, directly east of Cayo Tabona (Tavemier Key) just south of Key Largo. Then it would begin a series of zigzag tacks northward as the ships beat their way up the narrow Straits against the prevailing northeast winds.

Knowing how important it was for the fleet to reach the mouth of the Straits and pass through them without delay, generals Ubilla and Echeverz saw to it that the armada made good time. Their ships sailed hard during the day but more cautiously at night, the lookouts always within sight of the next ship's stern lantern or topmast. Despite the fleet's haste, its officers were wary, for charts were often wrong and the penalty for carelessness could be a collision with an unmarked reef.

At night the ships reduced sail and slackened their speed. Double lookouts were posted aloft and in the bows. Every fifteen to thirty minutes by the glass, soundings were made with a 300-foot deep-sea lead line. The ship's speed was determined by a log line—a block of wood (cast from the bow) on a 150-fathom rope divided into knots representing part of a league. The number of knots that ran out during one turn of a quarter-minute sandglass was multiplied to yield the distance the ship traveled in a given time.

By the early 18th century many ships carried a quadrant, but the earlier navigational instruments — the astrolabe and the cross-staff — were still in use for measuring the altitude of the sun or the polestar. The more accurate sextant and marine clock, so necessary for precisely determining longitude, had not yet been invented.

Compasses told the ship's direction, and a trickle of sand through hourglasses, turned every half hour by ship's boys, told the time. These were tended diligently day and night. The ringing of a bell from one to eight times with each successive turn of the watches marked the passage of time. Half of the working crew — often 50 to 100 men on the large ships — was on deck at all times. There were sails to be tended, rigging to be adjusted, lookouts to be kept, soundings to be taken, log lines to be cast, supplies to be shifted, pumps to be manned, repairs to be made, and the ship to be sailed. No one was ever idle. When there was nothing else to do, sailors swabbed decks, mended sails or made rope. Crews stood their watches twenty-four hours a day, each man alternating four hours on deck with four hours below. A sailor coming off watch crawled to his hammock on his hands and knees so as not to disturb sleepers in the other hammocks. It mattered little that his hammock was wet or that his clothes were damp, because in the darkness between decks, everything dripped. It dripped from the humidity and from the exhalations of closely packed creatures. It dripped because all wooden ships, in fair weather or foul, leaked badly above and below the waterline. Seawater constantly seeped through seams and splashed through ports, scuppers, hatchways and gunports. Closing the openings did little to stem the flow. Water ran in through upper-deck planks, streamed down cross beams and dripped on passengers below. Neither the ship nor the passengers ever dried out completely. Water that was not caught or absorbed ended in the bilges and had to be pumped regularly. From flooded bilges the ship reeked of drowned rats, rotting wood, decaying garbage, scummy ballast rock and foul bilge water. Stale food, sour bedding, wet clothes and unwashed people added to the overwhelming stench below decks. A pigsty would have smelled sweet by comparison. By the end of a long voyage the holds had to be fumigated with iron pots containing a smoking mixture of gunpowder, vinegar and water, or pans of burning pitch or brimstone. The treatment temporarily disguised but never entirely eliminated the smell.

Quite possibly it was these conditions that brought passengers up on the open decks as often as the weather and deck space permitted. On General Echeverz's flagship some of the men passed the time by trailing baited hooks over the side and catching sharks. The small fish were saved for eating. The large ones were either quickly dispatched or tormented for the amusement of the upper-class passengers by being thrown back into the water with a board tied to their tails. Other men gathered in the lee of the mainsails to talk and play cards while the women gossiped and sewed. The children ranged noisily and happily around the deck. When they were not helping the men catch sharks or plying the sailors with questions about sailing the ship, they were playing tag around the masts or teasing the animals in the stock pens.

Throughout the ship there were rigid fire regulations. Men were allowed to smoke only above the "waist," or forecastle, on the lee side of the ship, either day or night. Even there, their pipes had to be well covered or their cigars in holders. When the wind was strong, smoking was permitted only under the forecastle, where jars of water were placed for any emergency. Any violation of these orders brought severe penalties. Anyone caught smoking in an unauthorized area was put in iron bars with sliding fetters that shackled to the ankles and fed only bread and water for fifteen days. A seaman caught violating the smoking regulations was sentenced to a year's labor on the vessel without pay. As part of these same regulations, all fires aboard ship were to be extinguished before sunset, with the exception of well-covered lanterns. These alone were permitted above or below decks and were allowed to burn all night — one lantern before the door of each cabin, one at the entrance of the powder magazine but separated from it by a bulkhead, and another in the fore part of the ship between decks.

During the early part of the voyage, when provisions were abundant and fresh, everyone ate reasonably well. Breakfast might consist of boiled meal with molasses or flour dumplings fried in pork fat. On meat days, fresh fruit and vegetables were often served with Tassajos Fritos — sun- or wind-dried jerked beef. Other meals included a thick bean soup cooked with salt pork, and various meat and turtle stews. The choicest food was served to the officers and upper-class passengers, who often feasted on roast fowl, wine and honey. The usual after-dinner treat for everyone above the rank of common seaman was a mug of chocolate, a favorite beverage among the Spaniards since the conquest of Mexico, when Cortes's men inherited the bitter cacao bean drink from the Aztecs and discovered how good it was when sweetened. On fish days, boiled fish supplemented the meat, along with a kind of kidney bean soup called Mongos. Saucer-sized biscuits made of wheat flour and dried-pea flour served as bread. In the course of the voyage these weevil-ridden disks would become hard as rock and could be skipped across the water like flat stones. When there was an ample supply of water, the total daily ration was three pints. A shortage reduced the allotment to a small coconut shell full. This was all that was allowed for drinking or bathing.

Toward the end of a long sea voyage, meals were not so eagerly anticipated as they were in the beginning. Passenger Gemelli Careri's daily account of shipboard life on the Manila galleon during a crossing just seventeen years before the 1715 fleet's voyage explains why:

"The Ship swarms with little Vermin," he wrote, "the Spaniards call Corgojos, bred in the Biskit; so swift that they in a short time not only run over Cabbins, beds and the very dishes the Men eat on, but insensibly fasten upon the Body…. Abundance of Flies fall into the Dishes of Broth, in which swim Worms of several sorts…in every Mouthful there went down abundance of Maggots, and Corgojos chew'd and bruis'd. On Fish Days the common Diet was old rank Fish boil'd in fair water and Salt; at noon we had Mongos, something like Kidney Beans in which there were so many Maggots, that they swam at the top of the Broth, and the quantity was so great that besides the Loathing they caus'd, I doubted whether the Dinner was Fish or Flesh."

When the treasure galleons cleared the Double-Headed-Shot Keys between Cuba and the Bahamas, they caught the prevailing easterly winds blowing across the vast expanse of shoal water off their starboard side, known as the Great Bahamas Bank. While the vessels retained their ship-of-the-line formation that kept their cannon flanks clear, they tightened up, the lookouts warily watching the horizon for any sign of a strange sail. Privateers and Bahamian pirates openly roamed these waters, and the commanding generals were not taking any chances. News of the final peace in the recent war would be slow to reach all the participants, particularly some of the English privateers lurking in such far-flung colonial outposts as the Bahamas Islands. Indeed, some would purposely ignore the end of hostilities for a while in the hope of taking a final war prize. One could not be certain what might appear from behind the large islands over the horizon to the east.

If there was any apprehension among the passengers, it was not apparent. Their days were long and languorous. Under the hot tropical sun and the refreshing easterly breezes, the incredibly clear, deep blue water rolled by endlessly. And in those fathomless depths there were always strange, wonderful creatures to behold: flying fish erupting from the water ahead of the bows like flushing coveys of quail, gliding and skimming with their wing-fins spread; schools of smiling porpoises leaping and tumbling in the waves like playful children; big hump-headed dolphin fish the color of rainbows darting and flashing from beneath the frigate's hull, almost too quick to see; lazy loggerhead sea turtles the size of tubs, floating on the surface and staring curiously at the passing ships; fleets of purple air-bladders called Portuguese men-of-war sailing the waves; hundreds of lavender jellyfish as big as dinner plates floating in layers; and always, somewhere nearby, either following in the shade of the ship or trailing in her wake, the malevolent shadow of the shark.

Only at night, when the wind fell and the waves calmed, was there any change in the things to be seen and the things to be done. The sea grew dark and somber everywhere but around the slowly moving ships, where pale light flared in the water streaming past the bows and glowed green with phosphorescence in the gurgling wakes of the stems. Over this eerie phenomenon glittered the pale and wavering yellow lights of the ships' lanterns, somehow comforting, yet out of place on the lonely sea.

Entertainment in the evening was limited only by the passengers' talents and imaginations. In the pleasant downdraft of air from the big canvas sails, there was often singing and dancing aboard the treasure galleons. Impromptu plays, stunts, skits and buffoon shows were dramatically performed on the main deck for everyone's enjoyment. Or passengers might gather in the light of the lanterns to play "The Renegade Caxcara" and other innocent card games, all forms of gambling being prohibited. Toward the end of the voyage, after the ships had been at sea for nearly two months, there would come a day of joyous, unrestrained merrymaking. It was called the fiesta de las señas, a ceremonial occasion celebrating the first sighting of the "signs"—floating grass, sticks or other debris from land, or shore birds—that heralded their approach to land. The fiesta began sedately enough with the singing of a Te Deum, praising God for a safe crossing and an end to their wearisome journey. Then, to the accompaniment of drums and trumpets, everyone joined in an uproarious saturnalia (kept within the bounds of "decency and modesty") highlighted by a mock trial and punishment of ships' officers at the hands of the gleeful crews.

The flotilla finally reached Los Membros (Riding Rocks), on the northwest edge of the Great Bahamas Bank, where the fleet was to change course and head westward across the Straits to Florida. Until then, the northward progress of the treasure galleons had been uneventfully routine. By a rather devious course they had now reached 25°15' north latitude and had traveled some 150 nautical miles from Havana without mishap. Keeping well clear of the rocks, the ships swung one by one onto their new course and set out across the Straits.

At three o'clock that afternoon, the lookouts sighted white water over the Cape Reef, flanking the low-lying Florida Keys. Off Cayo Tabona, just south of Key Largo, the ships veered northward again. With the four-mile-an-hour Gulf Stream current pushing them, they beat their way up the coast, the overloaded frigates struggling to sail as closely as possible into the northeast winds, but managing not more than about a fifty-degree angle.

Finally the fleet reached the mouth of the Old Bahamas Channel, the beginning of the narrowest part of the Straits between the Florida shore and the Bahamas Bank, where the ships would start tacking northward. But now the winds grew erratic. First they blew strong from one quarter, fell off, then gusted from another. Frequently they died altogether. Sails slatted, tackle rattled and the vessels wallowed in the choppy, uncertain seas. No satisfactory course could be held under such conditions. General Ubilla chose to wait for better sailing weather.

For the next twenty-two hours the ships tacked back and forth well out at sea. Then about 2 P.M. the following afternoon, the winds settled more steadily into the northeast and the fleet started its journey up the Straits. Ships' officers

34

were kept busy watching for luffs in their sails and seeing that the crews leaped to their tasks with smartness and efficiency. Now, instead of going to whatever place work had to be done, each man of the watch had a special station. On the forecastle, an officer and two crewmen were in charge of handling the headsails and forward end of the ship. Another officer and two men in the waist of the vessel stood by to work the main tack and bowline, two others the foresheet and main. Other officers and men were responsible for seeing to the after yards and handling the lee fore and main braces, the main topsail, the topgallant and the weather cross-jack braces, while the rest of the watch stood ready at the main brace.

When the captain deemed the ship ready to tack, he gave the order, "Helm alee!" The helmsman pulled the wheel around, and the ship slowly turned into the wind. As she did, the officer on the forecastle shouted an order, and the headsail sheets were let go; then, in rapid succession down the full length of the ship, fore tack and main sheets were let go, and the opposite braces hauled — the weather cross-jack braces were belayed on one side and hauled on the other. From the foremast to the mizzenmast and from the gallants down, the yardarms swung around one after the other, the sails first fluttering and slapping, then filling and pulling taut, and finally being trimmed, with the sheets all made fast and the ship beating to windward again on a new angle. As long as the wind came from the same general direction, the ships could remain on the same tack for hours. Back and forth they sailed, first from within sight of the Florida shore eastward until the lookouts reported the bright green shoal water and sawtooth reefs of the Bahamas Bank; then, one after another, the vessels turned back on as much of a northwest course as they could muster against the northeast winds. As they sailed this zigzag course northward, each of the twelve vessels would tack once every three hours, night and day, for the next week.

On Sunday, July 28, the distance between ships gradually

widened as they moved up the passage. General Echeverz must have been annoyed to learn from his lookout that Captain Darie's frigate, the Grifon, had pulled out of line against orders and was now sailing well ahead and to the northeast of the fleet. Everyone knew that the brash young Frenchman had been forced to sail with General Ubilla's fleet from Vera Cruz to keep the Flota's sailing date a secret. And now the Frenchman was apparently showing his disdain for the slow-moving convoy by deliberately letting his ship take her head and pull away. It was an affront to Spain that Echeverz, an old knight, would not have taken lightly, but at the present there were more important things to worry about. On the south and southeastern horizon the rapidly growing banks of clouds had a strange, ominous quality about them. The evening sun sank into this somber setting, lining the western horizon hours before dark. Echeverz surely noted that the usually clear vial of shark oil, which he kept in his cabin to help him foretell the weather, was turning cloudy — a sure sign of approaching bad weather.

The next day — Monday, July 29 — offered no improvement. In the distance, to the leeward of the armada, lay the Florida coast, but even in the midday sun a strange milky haze obscured the view. The sea looked leaden. The ships rolled on long, steady swells sweeping toward shore. With each ungainly rising and falling, rudder pintles creaked, blocks clattered, rigging strained or slackened, and passengers braced themselves against the wild, inverted pendulum swing of the masts. Sailors who claimed they could feel the coming of bad weather in their bones complained of aching joints. Aboard the fleet's flagship, General Ubilla spent more time than usual on deck, staring eastward.

By Monday night, the prevailing wind had slackened noticeably, and a few rain squalls dotted the horizon. Instead of reducing sail, as was customary at night. General Ubilla ordered the fleet to lay on all canvas available. Foul weather was coming, and this was no place to delay. Both commanders

36

were well aware of their perilous position in the Straits and the danger of delay, but for the fleet's commanding general, Juan Ubilla, this realization undoubtedly was particularly poignant. From the inception of this combined fleet, there had been delays upon delays. Fateful delays. Each had seemed of little importance at the time. But now, on the night of July 29, 1715, if General Ubilla thought of anything other than how to avoid their impending problems with the worsening weather, the commander probably remembered all too clearly the unfortunate circumstances of the last three years that had brought them to their present predicament.

Chapter 3

Prelude to Disaster

Events that were to shape the destiny of the fleet began in 1712 during a period of historical turmoil near the end of the War of the Spanish Succession. This conflict, which stemmed from the accession of Phillip IV of Anjou, a Bourbon and grandson of Louis XIV of France, to the Spanish throne as Phillip V, had been a long and costly one for Spain and her French allies. Although their armies had acquitted themselves well in the European campaigns, the French and Spanish navies were less than successful in opposing the powerful English and Dutch fleets at sea. By controlling the seaways, particularly during the latter years of the war, the Anglo-Dutch fleets had effectively prevented Spain from drawing on the rich resources of her New World empire when she needed them most. After the enemy had destroyed seventeen Spanish treasure galleons at Vigo Bay in 1702 and captured the entire South American treasure fleet off Cartagena in 1708, Spain was understandably reluctant to risk any more large fleets in the Atlantic or Caribbean. Although some sailings continued during the war, these were usually limited to dispatch boats or small groups of vessels — nothing comparable to the large fleets, which had customarily carried on Spanish commerce in peacetime.

When it appeared that the war was coming to an end, however, Spain was anxious to pick up where she had left off. Even before the signing of the treaties at Utrecht in 1713, which officially ended the war. King Phillip V was moving to get the much-needed stored wealth from Spain's New World colonies. On March 3, 1712, he ordered the Council of the Indies to organize a flotilla of eight vessels to be ready to sail to New Spain. The king's directive was approved immediately in Madrid, and the powerful House of Trade at Seville, which controlled commerce and navigation in the Indies, began to enlist a Flota at the port of Cadiz.

It was not an easy job. When such fleets were organized in the latter part of the 16th century, there had been no difficulty in obtaining convoys of more than a hundred ships each to sail to the Spanish Indies; but now, in 1712, Seville was hard pressed to find even one ship to fill the order for a fleet to sail to Vera Cruz. Eventually, however, eight vessels were found for the voyage. An agreement was made on May 15, 1712, with Don Juan de Ubilla and Don Guyermo Con to prepare two of them as warships of 50 to 54 guns to serve in the New Spain fleet as Capitana and Almiranta. Ubilla, a veteran of many years' service in the Spanish fleets, became general. Since Guyermo Con declined to undertake the voyage, Don Francisco Salmon was named the admiral or Almiranta in his place.

The next few months were spent loading and provisioning the ships at Cadiz. In the cargo, the goods going to the New World were consignments of wine, brandy, olive oil, cloth, ironwork, books, two years' supply of officially letterheaded legal paper, and the royal monopoly of 3,999.5 hundredweight of mercury (just under 200 tons) to be used in the amalgam process for refining gold.

Although peace talks were under way by 1712, hostilities continued. General Ubilla was probably hesitant to risk the fleet while waters in Europe and the Western Hemisphere were still alive with enemy ships. Phillip V had ordered the Flota to sail by July 31, but it was delayed. On August 8 a report was brought to the general that five English warships of from 50 to 70 guns had been sighted near Cadiz. An armistice between England, France and Spain was signed on

August 19, 1712, but official word of this settlement was not published until September 4. Now the Council of the Indies decided that, regardless of risks, the fleet should sail. General Ubilla held a meeting of his major officers with representatives of the merchants' association. They voted that the fleet should sail, with three smaller vessels scouting ahead for any ships that might not have heard of the armistice.

As the day of departure approached, passengers began coming aboard. They were merchants, government officials with their families, bishops, friars, missionaries, people seeking their fortunes abroad, and an incredible number of hopeful opportunists who had bribed minor ships' officers to hide them as stowaways. And, as was always so, there were late arrivals.

Finally, after many lengthy delays, General Ubilla's fleet of eight vessels was ready to sail. The House of Trade officials had given the ships their final inspection to make certain that none carried unregistered cargo for which export taxes had not been paid, and the church officials had given their blessing to the fleet before it weighed anchor. Even then, there was one more last-minute delay. A wealthy nobleman and his entourage from Barcelona almost missed the ship because they had been held up by floods near Valencia. In addition, the portly gentleman was afflicted by gout in his feet and had to be carried aboard the Capitana in a sedan chair, which he controlled by applying his cane to the ribs of his lead porter. One hundred fourteen barrels of water had to be disembarked to make room for the new passenger's baggage. The Flota delayed sailing until early the next morning.

At 5:30 A.M. on September 16, the ships hoisted anchor and cleared from Cadiz — the two guard vessels leading the way, while the others fell in line behind General Ubilla's Capitana, the Nuestra Señora de la Regia. Admiral Salmon's Almiranta, the Santo Cristo de San Roman, brought up the rear.

The Marquis of Monroy was later to report in a letter to

the Council of the Indies that by 10 A.M. the fleet had rounded the point of Rota. As the wind freshened, the ships soon passed out of sight of land. "May God grant a fortunate voyage for this fleet," said the Marquis.

At sea the routine of the voyage began. Each member of the crew had specific jobs to do. The pilots attended to navigational matters, the seamen controlled the sails, the helmsmen steered the ships, and the ships' boys scrubbed the upper decks, fed the stock and took care of the wants of the officers and wealthy passengers. The entire crew took turns standing watches. Only the idle passengers had time on their hands.

As soon as the Flota was out of sight of land, it was discovered that there were 134 llovidos, or stowaways, aboard the flagship. These people had come aboard secretly, with the understanding that if they did not show themselves until the ship was far offshore, they would not be thrown into the water or allowed to die of hunger or thirst. To the Spanish way of thinking, a trip to the colonies practically guaranteed one's fortune; therefore the fleets sailing to the New World always had a large number of stowaways aboard. Spanish historian Cesareo Fernandez Duro reported that on one early-18th-century ship clearing from Cadiz with the Tierra Firma fleet, some three hundred stowaways who had "embarked secretly to travel on the King's money" were discovered.

As overcrowded as ships normally were, this should have created enormous logistics problems for the commanders, but apparently it did not. Although Spanish officials frowned on the practice, stowaways were accepted as a minor nuisance of the Indies trade.

The presence of these additional people aboard General Ubilla's flagship increased the total number to over eight hundred. Since most of the extra water supply had been disembarked to accommodate the last passenger's baggage, there was now more than a distinct possibility that there would be some thirsty stowaways aboard the Capitana before the fleet reached Vera Cruz.

As the days passed with monotonous regularity, the passengers amused themselves as best they could. Some fished for gilthead and sharks, while others made a game of watching the sky for rain clouds. With every small shower they spread pieces of cloth to catch the vital drops. Cockfights and mock bullfights were popular events. The latter never failed to draw a crowd to cheer for the "bull."

If the weather was pleasant in the evenings, there were other kinds of entertainment on the main deck beneath the great sails. On several occasions a troop of tumblers and jugglers, bound for the trade fairs, amazed and delighted everyone with their feats of agility and skill. There was also singing, recitations, and concerts with flute, violin and oboe. The Capuchin monks helped to lighten the spirits of those on board by holding a mission of nine days, a jubilee and general Communion. On General Ubilla's Capitana, moreover, there were two events uncommon to a warship: the wife of a prominent official en route to an important position in Vera Cruz presented her husband with their thirteenth offspring, and another woman gave birth to a healthy baby, but died in doing so.

For every death at sea, there was the ceremony of casting off the corpse, which ceremony the solemn and curious passengers always gathered to witness. While the priest performed his ritual, the crew stood at attention on deck; then with three shouts of "Bon voyage," the corpse was consigned to the deep. If scurvy or another deadly disease swept the ship, the ceremony was performed daily, and all the bodies were cast into the sea at once. At such times it is doubtful that the remaining passengers were much interested in watching these final rites being administered to their departed traveling companions.

Frequently the boredom of the voyage was broken by watching punishment metered out to someone for a crime or an infraction of the strict shipboard rules. Sometimes the offense was so minor that the punishment consisted only in making a man lie face down on the deck for a period of time. But for anything as severe as disobeying an order or stealing food or water from the supplies, the offender was beaten with a cat-o'-nine-tails. In all cases the captain-general of the ship decided the severity of the punishment—how many lashes should be applied, for example.

When the Flota reached the Canary Islands the two guard vessels left the fleet. General Ubilla sent two letters back to Spain on one of the ships, reporting that he had arrived there safely and was continuing.

Shortly after dawn on October 8, the Flota was about 250 leagues from Martinique in the West Indies when the lookout aboard the Nuestra Señora de la Regia sighted a sail on the western horizon. Now that the fleet no longer had its protective escort, the stranger's sudden appearance caused considerable apprehension until the vessel passed to leeward of the fleet and was identified as a French ship. In a letter to the Marquis de Monroy the French sea captain mentioned sighting the fleet. The Marquis in turn reported the event to the Council of the Indies in his letter of December 13, 1712.

In the diary of a passenger making that transatlantic voyage, we read that after more than a month at sea the overcrowded conditions, the ennui, the stinking squalor below decks and the rapidly diminishing food supplies began to tell on the passengers. Tempers flared, and petty grievances became the main topic of conversations. The irascible old nobleman from Barcelona complained that all he ever got to eat at the general's table was a thick corn soup and a perpetual stew of garbanzo beans. The ship's boy learned early to stay clear of the gouty old man when he was carried on deck in his sedan chair, for he often took out his temper on whoever was within reach of his cane. On several occasions he was seen to apply it rudely to the ribs of some of the pages and irreverently to the backsides of some of the bishop's relatives. According to accounts, another individual on board who was the recipient of wrath was the officer controlling the water ration. As the daily allotment grew smaller, the general resentment grew greater. No longer did the passengers call him by name; they simply referred to him as "the executioner of the thirsty." They said he was cruel, inexorable, incorruptible and given to argue even over the general's special orders dealing with the gouty old nobleman's chocolate mug. Before the voyage ended, the water officer would be thoroughly hated by all.

One day the first patache, the Nuestra Señora de las Nieves, began taking on more sea than usual through her teredo-riddled timbers, and the fleet stopped in midocean to make repairs. While divers went down to mend the hull, General Ubilla ordered a meeting aboard the flagship of all the ships' captains and pilots. The commander pointed out that since there was a shortage of drinking water, he wanted them to determine whether it would be feasible to sail for one of the Lesser Antilles and replenish their supply. The pilots got together and checked their navigation. Those from the Santissima Trinidad said they were 140 leagues from the islands. The chief pilot on General Ubilla's flagship set the distance at 135 leagues, and the second pilot at 100 leagues. With repairs completed, the fleet sailed on, but the discussions and debates about the pilots' accuracies continued until the islands had been passed.

The Flota stopped for water at San Juan, Puerto Rico, but passengers were not allowed ashore. The fleet then continued along the northern coast of the island, swung southwest through the Mona Passage and followed the southern coast of Hispaniola. In the latitude of Cabo Tiburon, General Ubilla opened his sealed orders and called another meeting of his fleet officers, in which everyone agreed that conditions seemed safe enough in the Indies for the convoy to go on to Mexico. The ships sailed along the southern coast of Cuba, crossing the Yucatan Channel to pick up Cabo Catoche, then stayed within sight of the Mexican mainland until they reached Vera Cruz on December 3.

The Flota anchored at the island of San Juan de Ulúa, directly opposite the town where a fort had been built to protect the fleets. Despite the importance of Vera Cruz as a New World trade terminus for Spain, the seaport was little more than a shantytown. Originally it had been located fifteen miles up the coast where Hernando Cortes and 508 conquistadors had first landed in 1519, but this was a poor choice. The open harbor was exposed in the winter to northern gales. Moreover, its entrance was blocked by a treacherous sandbar, which allowed the passage of small vessels but forced large ones to anchor at San Juan de Ulúa down the coast. Cargo was then transferred to smaller boats and brought to Vera Cruz. Finally, in 1599, the town was moved to its present location opposite the island. For almost two hundred years, Vera Cruz had dealt in the wealth that had enriched an empire, yet in 1712 it still looked like a transient town which wealth and progress had simply passed by. Since the trade fair would not be held until the following spring, Ubilla found the place virtually deserted. The general intended to winter his fleet there and get on with the business of discharging his cargo, selling it at the trade fair and loading for his outbound trip in the spring. But neither the commander nor the impatient king of Spain could have envisioned how long a delay fate was about to impose on the expedition.

A series of unfortunate incidents at Vera Cruz prevented the fleet's leaving for the next two years and five months. Although some of these events have been pieced together from official letters and documents of the period, they still present a fragmentary picture of the factors leading to the Flota's ultimate end.

Primarily, it appears that the Flota had trouble disposing of its cargo at the Vera Cruz trade fair in the spring. This was probably due to the presence of several French vessels that had special trade agreements with the Spanish king. The

French frigate Grifon arrived at Vera Cruz in May 1713 with three hundred tons of goods, which Captain Darie may have been able to sell at lower rates than Ubilla's, thereby making it more difficult for the commander to dispose of his merchandise. It is also possible that the Viceroy of New Spain was unprepared for the Flota's arrival and had not yet readied all the goods and treasure that would be going back to Spain. In any event, complications delayed the fleet through the summer and into the fall hurricane months of 1713, when it would have been unwise for the Flota to try to reach Havana.

On May 18, 1714, officials of the House of Trade complained to the Crown that Seville was badly in need of funds. They said they had twice received word that the fleet would sail by February after needed repairs, but that it had not. Consequently, the House of Trade tribunal went unpaid, and there were back charges on the fleet's revenues owing since 1711.

In September the fleet was damaged by a storm at Vera Cruz and so required further delay for repairs. On December 8 the Council of the Indies reported to the king that Ubilla's fleet had twice been ready for loading, but the outbound cargo was still in the warehouses. Once again the star-crossed fleet was forced to winter in Vera Cruz.

By spring of 1715, however, the Flota was finally being loaded. Most of the Mexican treasure consisted of 1714 silver coinage. The viceroy had ordered the mints into overtime operation that year so that the fleet could carry back to Spain as much silver as the Mexican mines had produced up to then. The entire process, from mining to minting, had been slow and laborious. In previous centuries the rich veins had been closer to the surface, where the high-grade ore was easier for the Indian slaves to obtain. But by the 18th century, some of these mines had become as deep as nine hundred feet; the risks were greater, the accident rate was higher, and the grade of ore was poorer. Working in these narrow, dangerous mine shafts under the worst conditions, the Indians hammered the ore loose from the surrounding rock, hauled it to the surface in baskets and crushed it into fine powder for refining. Prior to the 1555 discovery of the amalgamation process in which mercury was used to simplify the refining of precious metals, powdered ore was mixed with lead and carbon, placed in crucibles and melted over wood fires fanned by large bellows. The lead and impurities were skimmed off with ladles, and the liquid silver was poured into molds to solidify. But with the amalgamation process, the powdered ore was nixed with mercury to separate the precious metal from the impurities. The silver and mercury amalgam was then cooked until the mercury evaporated and only the silver remained. This was either left as wedges or remelted and poured into round disks or bars. These were inspected by an assayer who either passed them as an acceptable grade of silver, cutting a mint or mine-owner's mark into the surface, or returned them for additional refining. Up to 20 percent of the precious metal mined, often called the "Royal Fifth," was subtracted as the Crown's share. Since mercury was indispensable to the refining process, the Crown monopolized the Empire's entire production of this metal and furnished it to the New World mines from the Empire's two major mercury mines, one in Almaden, Spain, and the other in Huancavelica, Peru.

Actually very little silver was sent to Spain as bullion. That an accurate inventory of the precious metal being purified and sent home might be kept, most of it went to one of the mints to be converted into coinage. In this process, pieces of silver the approximate size and weight of the intended coins were clipped or chiseled from the ends of flat strips of silver. These were then hand struck between two dies, which embossed them with the cross of Spain on one face and the royal coat of arms on the other. Although the handmade dies carried the date, the coins were minted so carelessly that the date seldom showed on the finished coin. The most important thing was that the coin be of the right weight and purity; consequently it was desirable to show the mint mark and assayer's initial. All silver coins were called reals and during this period were struck in denominations of 1, 2, 4, and 8 reals—the largest denomination being known as a piece of eight. The irregularities of the strip gave each cob coin an angular, irregular shape, and no two were exactly alike. The crude coins were probably reminted in Spain. In the early 18th century, a piece of eight (or 8 reals) was often a peso, a monetary unit which at that time had a purchasing power equal to about $12 in our present currency; 9,000 pesos could buy a ship complete with crew and supplies.

Essentially similar refining and minting processes were used for gold, except that the weight was watched far more closely. If the gold was minted into coins, they were called escudos through the 18th century and doubloons from that period on. Doubloons were minted in the same denominations as silver coins, but they were struck more precisely. Since gold was worth approximately sixteen times the same weight of silver, the purchasing power of gold.

In the early 18th century, one silver real, the equivalent of 12 1/2 cents, could buy so many groceries in the Mexico market that the purchaser needed a cart to carry them home. An 8-escudo gold doubloon in the early 18th century was equal to approximately $200 in today's currency.

The Audencia, New Spain's colonial council, had tentatively set the date for the Flota's departure for Havana in late March. Following this decision the officials, as required by law, halted the issuance of licenses permitting other vessels to leave Vera Cruz before the Flota sailed. This was done to prevent knowledge of the exact sailing date of the treasure fleets from falling into the hands of pirates or belligerents who might capture small or lightly armed merchant vessels and force this information out of those aboard.

One of the vessels detained by the closing of the port was the French warship Grifon, commanded by Captain Darie. Early in 1712, when it became obvious that peace was imminent, Darie had applied for and received—as indicated above—a special license to trade with New Spain. These special trade permits granted to the French by the Crown were apparently a natural outgrowth of the two countries' wartime alliance and the fact that Spain was gradually losing the trade monopoly she had always enjoyed with her New World possessions. Captain Darie had paid the considerable sum of 50,000 pesos (equal to about $600,000 today) for the license, and he was understandably annoyed at not being allowed to get his merchandise back to France—especially since he could reasonably expect a profit return of from four to eight times his original investment in fees and cargo.

With his ship nearly loaded and ready to go, Darie appealed to the Audencia to make an exception in his case. He argued that an unnecessary layover would cause additional expenses to himself and other investors; that since his vessel was a warship it was unlikely to be a target for pirates; and finally, that he was a French national, and the ruling applied only to Spanish subjects.

The council turned a deaf ear to his appeal. He was told that the Grifon could either sail with the fleet or sometime after. Darie reluctantly agreed to accompany the fleet.

Early in March, when it became apparent that the fleet would not be ready to leave on time, a new date, April 11, was set for sailing. Then on March 28, when the ships were about half loaded, a particularly violent storm struck Vera Cruz. Hurricane-force winds swept across the exposed harbor and hurled twelve ships against the coast, smashing them to pieces or holing their hulls. Two ships of the Flota, one of the pataches and another small vessel, were lost.

The second patache pitched and rolled and came out badly damaged. The Urca de Lima, which had become the fleet's resfuerzo, snapped one of her cables and ended up six leagues away from her mooring with several broken timbers. It took eleven days to return the vessel to her position. The Capitana was blown from her mooring and ran into a reef, and General Ubilla ordered the masts chopped down to save the lives of those aboard. The ship managed to drop anchor and remain afloat. Both the Grifon and another French warship, the Francaise, snapped their cables and drifted. Darie's men got the Grifon anchored again, but the ship was badly shaken. The Francaise drifted off so far that she left the other vessels behind. Only the Almiranta, sheltered by the fortress of San Juan de Ulúa, escaped undamaged.

The Flota was now forced to lay over another five weeks for repairs and final loading. If this unfortunate turn of events rankled. General Ubilla kept the fact to himself. What the commander could not foresee, however, was that four months and three days later, this and previous delays would be largely responsible for troubles that would confront his fleet in the Florida Straits.

Finally, on May 4, 1715, the Flota sailed from Vera Cruz for Havana, accompanied by the French ship, Grifon. After the storm losses, the fleet was down to four vessels, the Capitana, the Almiranta, the resfuerzo and the patache of Soto Sanchez. These ships were heavy-laden with treasure, most of it aboard the two well-armed warships, the Capitana and the Almiranta. They alone carried the king's treasure, 1,222,824 pesos 3 tomines 5 grains in silver coins and bullion. In addition, General Ubilla's flagship, the Nuestra Señora de la Regia, carried 8,076 small chests and sacks of silver coins comprising privately registered treasure, plus sixty- two chests of gifts and one small chest of gold bars, doubloons and pearls. There were also considerable amounts of worked silver, cochineal, indigo, vanilla, chocolate, copper, Chinese porcelain, brazilwood, balsam and other miscellaneous cargo.

Besides the royal treasure, Admiral Salmon's Almiranta, the Santo Crista de San Roman, carried 2,076,004 pesos in silver for private interests, plus 684 small chests and sacks of gifts, Chinese porcelain, worked silver and other less valuable riches. The resfuerzo, the Urca de Lima, carried 252,171 pesos of privately registered silver, and the patache, the Nuestra Señora de las Nieves, carried 44,000 pesos in coined silver and bullion.

The Flota sailed northward with the winds and the current into the Gulf of Mexico, following the coast on a course that more than a month later would bring the vessels to Havana and the long- awaited rendezvous with the Galeones fleet of General Echeverz.

Meanwhile, the Galeones de Tierra Firma, waiting for the Flota in Cuba, had had far less difficulty keeping to its schedule. In 1712, while the Flota was being enlisted at Cadiz, the king granted registries for a fleet of privately owned vessels to sail to Cartagena and pick up the treasure of South America. These contracts to civilians were issued in the name of Don Antonio de Echeverz, Don Manuel Lopez Pintado and a few other influential speculators. The fleet consisted of four vessels, the Nuestra Señora del Carmen, Echeverz's flagship; the Nuestra Señora del Rosario, his Almiranta; and two pataches, the Nuestra Señora de la Concepcion and the El Señor San Miguel. In the contract signed June 23, 1713, Echeverz agreed to take 1,000 quintales of mercury, 150 troops and 471 packets of sealed paper to the New World, returning in one year with all the silver, gold and royalties from the South American mainland for the Crown loaded aboard his flagship.

Ubilla's Flota had left Cadiz in September 1712. Echeverz was ordered to leave the following spring — in May 1713 — but as usual there were delays in preparing the ships for departure. When the vessels were not ready by mid-May, the sailing date was moved to June 3. The spring floods that ravaged Spain that year, making it difficult to obtain food supplies, caused further delay. Finally, the ships were loaded and sailed from Cadiz on July 9, 1713. Most of the cargo they carried was general trade supplies, including hundreds of tons of English manufactured goods, books, cloth, wax, ironwork and nails. There was the usual livestock brought along for food during the voyage, but General Echeverz had got out of carrying several camels aboard the Capitana. Although the animals were to have been sent to the Marquis de Villarocha, president of the High Court of Panama, with the intention of acclimating them to serve as replacements for mules used to transport silver and other cargo across the Isthmus, they would now have to go by another fleet.

With the signing of the last treaties at Utrecht that year, war tensions eased and the galleons sailed westward across the Atlantic without an additional escort and without mishap. Once they entered the Caribbean and were following the warm westerly currents off the Lesser Antilles, General Echeverz sent one of his pataches, the El Señor San Miguel, on to Havana to purchase in advance the large amount of tobacco he intended to pick up there the following year. The remaining three ships maintained their course along the north coast of South America, sighting their landmark at Cabo de la Vela and sailing southwestward past Cabo de la Aguija and Santa Marta, where the voyagers offered their prayers of thanks for a safe crossing to the sanctuary of the Virgin Mary built high in the hills. On August 29, after fifty days at sea, the galleons sailed through the narrow Boca Chica pass into the fine ten-mile-long harbor at Cartagena, New Granada.

Ever since its founding in 1533, this important port on the northern coast of present-day Colombia had been the first stop for most of the ships in the Tierra Firma Armadas coming to the New World. Officially it was called Cartagena de las Indies to differentiate it from the port of Cartagena on the Mediterranean in southeastern Spain. Within two years after the Caribbean town was founded, it was actively engaged in the shipping business. Although other ports along the Spanish Main were closer to the routes used to transport gold and emeralds from the interior, none offered such an excellent harbor as Cartagena. The harbor is formed by an indention of the coastline enclosed by two long islands lying parallel to the mainland. Originally there were two entrances—the Boca Grande (large mouth) and the Boca Chica (small mouth). The more than ten-mile-long harbor with its two entrances could easily shelter hundreds of ships. The only disadvantage was that entry was so easy that Cartagena was attacked and sacked three times by sea-rovers before the Spanish got around to building adequate defenses.

Considering the seaport's past, it is understandable that the port resembled a veritable armed fortress when General Echeverz and the galleons arrived there in 1713. The town, about three-quarters of a mile long and half a mile wide, was surrounded by a heavy wall, in places forty feet thick. Several formidable-looking forts, including the turreted battlements of Fort San Felipe, stood ready to defend it.

The arrival of the Tierra Firma fleet at Cartagena was the big event of the year. It heralded the forthcoming trade fair, the long- awaited feria, with its special emphasis on business and pleasure.

As soon as the ships were moored and the official preliminaries over, General Echeverz dispatched a boat northwestward across the Gulf of Darien to the small town of Porto Bello, to carry the news that the fleet was in. The intelligence was sent by courier across the Isthmus to the president of Panama, who relayed it by boat to Peru so that the gold and silver shipment could be started north. To make certain that Peru got the word, native runners were also sent overland with the message to the viceroy at Lima.

For the next two months the galleons remained in Cartagena. Cargo was disembarked for the port, fresh water and victuals were taken aboard, and a small boat was sent to collect the annual pearl harvest at the island of Margarita off the coast of present-day Venezuela. When Echeverz learned that the treasure shipment from Peru had reached Panama City and was being transported across the Isthmus for the annual trade fair at that port, the fleet weighed anchor on November 4 and sailed to Porto Bello.

In the early 18th century this small Caribbean seaport on the Isthmus of Panama was both uncomfortable and unhealthful. The intense heat, the encroaching jungle and the prevalence of tropical fevers made it a difficult place to live, especially for unacclimatized foreigners. Originally the main trade terminus on the Isthmus had been Nombre de Dios, a small town several miles up the coast. But this unwalled settlement had a shallow, hazardous harbor and such a high mortality rate from tropical fever that it was called the "Graveyard of the Spaniards." Although Nombre de Dios was close to Panama City and the treasure traffic from the south, conditions were so bad there that Phillip II ordered the town moved to its present site at Porto Bello, which after 1596 became the main port of call on the Isthmus for the Tierra Firma Fleets. Though Porto Bello did have a better harbor, the move did not change the sultry climate or cut down the fever fatalities.

To visitors and citizens alike, however, these matters were of little concern once the Porto Bello trade fair began. Rum flowed freely, merriment was the order of the day, and business was brisk in the shade of the great sailcloth tents erected in the city square. The fleet remained in Porto Bello through the winter, and on April 24, 1714, with the ships heavy-laden with goods and treasure, it returned to Cartagena, arriving there on May 15. During its stay some of the ships had sailed in patrol of the local coast and had had the good fortune to overtake and capture two foreign vessels engaged in smuggling. One was the French frigate El Ciervo, which General Echeverz renamed La Galeria; the other was a Dutch sloop. La Holendesa, which he renamed the San Miguel. The crews were taken prisoner and the vessels added to the fleet.

Through the summer months the remaining treasure and goods for Spain were loaded aboard the ships. Finally, on September 7, when the fleet cleared for Havana, General Echeverz's Capitana was carrying 7,766 pounds of cacao beans for making cocoa and chocolate; 33,600 pounds of brazilwood; 79,967 pesos 22 reals in gold bars and doubloons; 309

castellanos; 7 tomines; 6 grains of gold dust; 18 marks of gold; 5 1/2 ounces of silver; 1,175 pesos 8 reals of plata doble, and three gold chains worth 380 pesos 14 reals. The Almiranta carried 15,514 pesos 13 1/2 reals in gold bars and doubloons, 175 pesos in plata doble, chests of gifts and general cargo, which included brazilwoods, cacao, dry goods and hides. Along with similar goods the merchant nao, the Nuestra Señora de la Concepcion, carried 8,503 pesos 3 reals in gold bars and doubloons. The remaining ships were to be loaded in Havana.

The Galeones reached this Cuban port on October 2, 1714. It was too late in the year to expect General Ubilla and the Flota from Vera Cruz. However, Havana was a far better place than Cartagena to winter the fleet. It had a well-defended deep-water harbor capable of sheltering hundreds of ships, the balmy climate was agreeable to Europeans, and in the early 18th century this fast-growing city of almost 50,000 was a far cry from the primitive settlements at the other ports of call along the Caribbean.

As the early months of 1715 passed, General Echeverz loaded 1,500,000 pounds of tobacco aboard his ships while he impatiently awaited the Flota. Then, a month after it arrived, the combined flotilla sailed.

If either commander had any foreboding of doom in those final days of July as the fleet pushed on through the treacherous Florida Straits under threatening skies, he undoubtedly kept his fears to himself. But the prelude was over. It was the beginning of the end.

Chapter 4

The Sea Came Like Arrows

On Tuesday, July 30, dawn broke on an oppressively hot, humid day. People's hands felt clammy; their clothes stuck to their bodies. The fleet had made little progress during the night. Winds were erratic, often changing directions, sometimes ceasing to blow at all. During these lulls the creaking rigging of distant vessels could be heard over the water. The sun seemed enveloped in thin yellowish gauze. The unceasing swells grew larger and the ships rolled with more abandon. By noon there was not a man, woman or child in the fleet who did not sense that there was grave trouble ahead.

Gradually the wind picked up out of the northeast. The ships leaned into the steepening waves, but their northward movement was slow and awkward. Much time was lost on long southeastward runs necessary to gain sea room to tack northward along the coast. Shreds of grayish clouds scudded across the sky, gathering in an ominous black mantle that blotted out the sun. The wind blew increasingly stronger; the waves grew foaming crests. Pilots conferred with their captains to decide the best tactics to follow. If they reduced sail too much, they might lose valuable sea room and end up on the Florida shore. Yet if they did not reduce sail and were suddenly hit by high winds, they might lose both sails and upper masts. Ubilla's decision aboard the Capitana of the Flota was to reduce sail. Aboard Echeverz's flagship the proper signals were made and both watches were called out.

Hatches and ports were closed and battened down. The crow-jack yard was lowered and reefs taken in the topgallants.

By midafternoon it had grown so dark that stern lanterns were lighted. Sporadic rain squalls lashed the fleet, the heavy downpours completely obscuring the ships. Suddenly the wind veered to the east and shrieked across the Straits at forty knots, wind across current — an awful combination to sail in. The rolling, rushing water thrust up jagged peaks that the gale instantly whipped into white spindrift and foam, driving it across wave troughs to mottle and streak the angry gray-black sea like veined marble.

With the storm's first powerful blast, the ships staggered and heeled over sharply. Sheets of spray blanketed the bows, spurted from around closed gunports, hawseholes and scuppers to race wildly across the decks. The ships no longer obeyed their helms but were forced around into the wind, righting as they swung bows on into the weather. Headsails flogged violently; standing and running rigging thrummed like strings on a giant harp. With a hissing rush, a solid wall of rain advanced on the fleet, the wind-driven drops hammering the foaming seas so hard that they seemed to smoke. Crews were ordered aloft to furl the topgallant sails. Shielding their faces against the stinging fury of the squall, the men clawed their way to the ratlines and climbed upward into the howling black nightmare where ropes, yards, tackle and sails thrashed, slapped, banged and clattered in wild confusion. The rain and the wind tore at their flimsy jackets and duck trousers. Attempts at speech were impossible, for words were whipped from lips and drowned in the shattering discord. Hand over hand the men went out on the swaying yards 130 feet above the dizzying deck, going by feel alone, their feet sliding along a single slippery wet rope arcing through space while they gripped the thick yard with fishhook fingers and knew that a single missed grip or misstep would send them plummeting into eternity. The driving rain seemed determined to pin them to their swaying perches in the sky, while the sharp wind tried to scrape them off. There was no such thing as turning their faces to windward, for the weather pounded them mercilessly from all sides. With outstretched arms they tried to smother the violently flapping sails, clutching and pulling canvas to them, getting it halfway in, only to have it ripped from their grasp, but grabbing again with fingers numb from fatigue, and fighting it in. Finally the sails were bunched on the yards and gaskets passed over them as snugly as possible before the men slid down the shrouds to the deck. For some there was a few minutes' rest; for others it was forty minutes on the pumps, trying to keep the already excessive volume of water in the bilges under control.

Half the watch went below, where there was little more comfort than in the hell they had just left. Down the full length of the gun deck, upper beams rained steady streams of water on the miserable folk huddled row after row in their soggy hammocks. Children cried, the devout or terrified prayed, the sick moaned. And now the stifling air had another overpowering odor added to it: the stench of vomit.

At least the wet hammocks offered some small relief, for their swaying was far less violent than that of the rest of the ship, whose decks, bulkheads, timbers, knees and beams were in constant motion, tilting forward and back and rolling from side to side, sometimes the parts working against one another in agonizingly shrill discord. Below decks the whole ship creaked, groaned or screamed in torment. To this was added the muffled sliding, scraping and bumping of shifting cargo, the jolting thunder of bows crashing into waves, the hiss and gurgle of water rushing past the hull, the thud and rattle of tackle dropping on the deck overhead, and the screeching of the rows of cannon straining at their lashings along both sides of the gun deck.

The weary sailors had hardly slumped into their hammocks when there was a sudden sharp, booming explosion topside, as if a 24-pounder had fired, then a banging on the scuttle and a cry for all hands on deck. The men scrambled for the ladder and stumbled back out into the storm. The fore-topsail had split from clew to earing and was blowing to pieces. The first watch was already aloft, fighting to control the topgallants that had blown free from the gaskets and were streaming loose from the yards.

Once again the men climbed up into the reeling darkness of thrumming rigging and careening yardarms. It took more than a half hour to drag in the tattered sail and furl it around the yard, lashing it with double gaskets and tightening the rolling tackle until it looked like a crudely bandaged broken limb.

Two hours later the rain passed as quickly as it had come, but the wind moved into the northeast and blew harder, gusting to fifty knots. Mountainous white waves crashed over the bows. The men were aloft constantly in their endless battle against the wind and the sails. Officers strained to see the arcing amber glow of lanterns on the vessels ahead and behind as the specks of light rose, lurched and disappeared behind the heavy seas. The commanders knew that the worst was yet to come. If they had not been caught in the channel between the Bahamas Bank to the east and the inhospitable Florida coast to the west, they could have run south or southwest, away from the storm. But they were trapped unless the wind shifted. Although they could not maintain sail in the rising winds, their only hope was to go on, to try to pass what is now Cape Canaveral rather than collide with it at the mercy of a full-blown hurricane.

By midnight the fleet had been pounded by five vicious gales, each worse than the one before. Safety lines stretched fore and aft kept the watches from washing overboard as they went to and from the rigging, but the strain of fighting the storm had already left its mark on the ships and the men. All the vessels had badly opened seams; water rose in the holds. Pumps had to be manned constantly. Two seamen had fallen from swaying yards on Ubilla's Capitana and been lost at sea. The general's Almiranta had to jury-rig a mainsail, the first two having been blasted to shreds during the squalls. Echeverz's Capitana had lost its jib-boom and part of its bowsprit from plowing into the unyielding seas. With them the topgallant mast and sails had crashed down and enveloped the forecastle, part of the debris dragging in the water until it was slashed free and allowed to go by the board. There was no hope of repair. Each time the flagship's bows went under, tons of water were scooped up and flung across the forecastle onto the maindeck. Trunks, bales, barrels, livestock—everything washed about in confusion. Yet, somehow, each time the vessel managed to pull her head free, to rise up out of the foaming abyss with water gushing from her scuppers, the deck cargo settled momentarily into a new pattern of disorder, until the ship plunged down again into the next onrushing wall of water.

Having failed to finish the fleet with its first vicious onslaughts, the storm grew worse. The wind blew harder, the waves piled higher, the rain came in torrents. The ships were now completely out of control. General Echeverz's Capitana shipped a sea at her stern that almost finished her. It blasted in the cabin windows and bulkheads of the poop, sending tons of water rushing through the officers' quarters and down companionways, the blow knocking pilots and officers off their feet on the deck just above. The last sails tore loose from their gaskets and split open. Sailors aloft did what they could to jury-rig the remains, but it was already too late.

At 2:00 A.M., Wednesday, July 31, the hurricane struck with all its fury, roaring out of the east with winds in excess of seventy-five miles an hour. Nothing withstood its wrath. One moment jury sails were bowed rock hard from their improvised yards; the next instant they were gone, atomized, the sounds of their passing no more heard above the howling holocaust than the crash of splintered masts or the screams of maimed men. The air was filled with foam, the wind-driven spray flying like arrows. Once recognizable waves were now towering white moving Matterhorns of destruction that overwhelmed and crushed whatever ships they encountered, while pushing others inexorably closer to the seething maelstrom of water thundering over the Florida shoals.

The fleet was helpless; each ship was on its own. Some wallowed broadside to the waves and the wind. The land was near. Dismasted ships broached to, touched bottom and were tom apart, every living thing swept away. On other vessels the end took longer, and there was time for prolonged pandemonium. Crazed livestock reared and plunged on decks littered with men trying to free themselves from fallen rigging. People driven by fear swarmed out from below decks into the black tumult of destruction and added to the confusion. Ships that survived the moment were given but a temporary reprieve. But in those moments, crews drew on the last reserves of mind and limb in an effort to try to save their vessels by jettisoning cargo, cannon and anchors and frantically slashing away rigging that had already gone by the board, its weight threatening to drag the ships over on their beam ends.

On General Ubilla's flagship, the Nuestra Señora de la Regia, the crew tried to chop down the masts, hoping to lighten ship enough to let it float closer to dry land, for if the vessels could not save themselves by avoiding the shoals, their only hope was to reach shore to save lives. But for the big Capitana it was too late. The 471-ton vessel struck bottom with such force that her entire lower hull was sheared away. Ballast, cargo, cannon, passengers and 120 tons of registered silver coins in boxes plummeted to the bottom of the rampaging sea, while the superstructure continued shoreward, breaking up as it went. General Ubilla, commander of the armada, and some 220 others drowned.

Santo Cristo de San Roman, the 450-ton Almiranta of the Flota, also lost the lower part of her hull after striking bottom; the upper works broke to pieces near shore. One hundred twenty persons drowned. Two of the Plata's tenders, Ubilla's recently purchased small frigate and the Nuestra Señora de las

Nieves were literally tom apart in the surf. On the former, twelve persons perished; on the latter, two dozen drowned as the deck lifted off the hull, but some one hundred survivors rode the wreckage ashore like a raft. The Flota's supply ship, the Santissima Trinidad, called the "Urca de Lima," was the only vessel to remain virtually intact. Although she lost her foremast, her crew managed to anchor her between two rock ledges lying parallel to the shore near the mouth of a river. In trying to reach shore, thirty-five drowned. The Urca remained afloat until eight o'clock that evening, when a second violent storm caused the seas repeatedly to lift and drop the vessel on her own foremast tangled underneath until she holed her hull and sank on the spot. General Echeverz's flagship, the Nuestra Señora del Carmen, was more fortunate than the other large warships. The crew lightened her sufficiently for the vessel to reach the shallows near shore, where she sank, listing, but with little loss of life. General Echeverz was among the survivors. His Almiranta, the Nuestra Señora del Rosario, was totally destroyed near shore a little farther south; 124 perished, including her captain, General Echeverz's son.

In a few short hours the hurricane took its terrible toll on the Spanish treasure fleet of 1715. Eleven vessels, more than 14 million pesos of registered treasure, and seven hundred lives were lost in one of the worst sea disasters in history. Of the twelve ships that sailed from Havana, only one escaped — the French frigate Grifon, whose captain, Don Antonio Darie, had slowly pulled away from the fleet and was sailing so far to the northeastward at the time of the disaster that he was out of the hurricane's path. In fact, when he reached Europe, he was unable to report that there had even been a storm! When the fleet failed to appear off the Carolina capes where it would sail east for Spain, Darie, who had waited several days at that latitude, thought the ships had simply been delayed by a "prolonged calm."

Chapter 5

Castaways in the Land of the Ays

The hurricane was so severe and turbulent that, according to what he heard from old sailors, they had never seen one like it. Such was the violence of the sea waves that they seemed like arrows even to those on land, so that many who managed to reach the shore also were killed. It is calculated that more than 600 other persons drowned or were missing from all the ships in these coasts and beaches, with the added misfortune that, after some of the ships and part of the cargo of others had been washed ashore, the furious swaying to and fro of the sea waves would drag everything back into the ocean, where it disappeared, so that the coast was bare again.

From the deposition of Father Francisco
de Leon y Cabrera, August 12, 1715

For the next eight hours the wind and the rain tore at the coast, the waves thundered into the beaches, and, to the south, one ship after another smashed upon the shoals. The living, the dying and the dead were cast up indiscriminately on the beach, along with broken planks, shattered timbers, tangled rigging, boxes, barrels, chests, and anything else that the capricious waves spared. Wreckage and people were scattered for almost thirty miles along the bleak, uninhabited coast. Wherever a ship was crushed between surf and shoals, the tragic flotsam washed ashore. Most of the women and children never made it. Neither did some of the seamen, who, though good swimmers, sank like bar-shot, their pockets bulging with the heavy silver coins rifled from passengers' baggage or from the boxes of treasure carried aboard ship. Dazed and disoriented survivors whose lives had been spared by the sea crawled up the narrow strip of sand to face the nightmare of the storm on land. Many stumbled over each other in their scramble up the dunes to the scrub palmettos and palms. Others, lost and confused in the dark, too exhausted or injured to drag themselves away from the water's edge, stayed where the waves had washed them. The sea was impartial. Whoever was unable to move out of its reach was swept back into oblivion.

At daybreak the beach was strewn with wreckage and bodies. Other bodies tumbled grotesquely in the waves with waterlogged barrels, bales and debris. There was no sail on the horizon. All one saw was grim skies, heaving seas and the terrible evidence of what had happened. Survivors later reported seeing seamen on the beach bent over bodies as if searching them for signs of life. But that was not what they were looking for. They were robbing the dead of rings and valuables. Others were observed eagerly pulling clothing out of a large trunk, until some officers and marines came down from the dunes and made them stop. After a while the seamen began dragging some of the boxes and barrels into a pile well above the tide line. The bodies were laid in rows below the dunes and covered with torn sails. Several seamen collected wood and started a fire on the beach. As the wind slackened, more people left the palmettos, and a large group soon gathered around the fire.

This scene was repeated in nine other places along the narrow barrier island that parallels the southeast Florida mainland from what is now Cape Canaveral to a point south of present-day Fort Pierce. This region was known to the Spanish as Palmar de Ays, or palm grove of the Ays, named for some two thousand troublesome Ays Indians who lived along the mainland in this area. Since the survivors were uncertain just how hostile the Ays might be, they were wary of venturing any farther into the island than the sand dunes. In the first few hours after the worst of the storm had passed, they were unable to do much more than care for their injured and bury their dead, scratching shallow graves in the white sand to be blessed as a matter of course by surviving priests. Then they took what comfort they could from the driftwood fires they built on the beach.

That evening at eight o'clock, a second violent storm sank the Urca de Lima, aground near the mouth of the old Indian River inlet, the only vessel that had remained afloat.

Now only her maindeck showed above water. Although the longboats and some provisions had been taken off before she filled with water, most of the supplies were still in her flooded hold. A similar situation existed several miles to the north, where General Echeverz's Capitana had come to rest near a sand point. The few perishable provisions that had not been swept overboard during the storm only tantalized the hungry survivors camped on the beach opposite the wreck. However, these people and those near the Urca fared far better than survivors at the other camps, who found that most of the provisions had either gone down with their ships or had been swept away from the beach by the strong coastal currents. They were lucky to get some water from the few casks and bamboo containers that drifted ashore to slake their thirst temporarily.

But at least one good thing came of the night: the realization that they were not alone, that there were other fires and probably other survivors scattered along the distant beach.

At the southernmost wreck of the fleet, where the Flota's patache, the Nuestra Señora de las Nieves, had gone down. Captain Soto Sanchez took a careful fix on the wreck's latitude with a quadrant he had salvaged, and determined that he and his companions were 137 miles south of the only civilization in these parts — the Spanish settlement at St. Augustine. After sending a sergeant and two seamen down the coast a way to see if there were any other wrecks, and learning that there were no survivors in that direction, Sanchez immediately started leading his party north along the beach to find the commanding officers of the devastated fleet.

Four miles up the coast, on the south side of the inlet, the Sanchez group met Captain Miguel de Lima and his men, who were preparing to burn off the upper deck of the Urca so that they could haul up valuable provisions stored inside the supply ship's flooded hold. Two of the vessel's longboats had been salvaged, and although they were in need of repair, Don Miguel assured Sanchez that they would soon be made serviceable enough to help transport injured passengers and provisions.

At Sand Point, near present-day Rio Mar, survivors from General Echeverz's Capitana, the Nuestra Señora del Carmen, were busy salvaging what they could from the badly damaged ship that had sunk near shore. The vessel was listing, but her upper works were still out of water and relatively intact. Carpenters hoped to repair one of her large launches, which had not been claimed by the waves. As yet no attempt had been made to salvage any of the waterlogged provisions from inside the wreck.

That afternoon a runner arrived from the north with the news that General Ubilla was dead and that his admiral, Francisco Salmon, second in command of the Flota, was now in charge. Admiral Salmon sent word that the remaining officers were to organize their people and move them up the beach to his camp at the Bara de Ays.

Throughout this period everything was totally disorganized. Some looting was occurring at all the camps opposite each wreck along the coast. Those mainly involved were seamen and lower-class passengers. Risking no more than a reprimand from ships' officers who were largely unarmed and vastly outnumbered, the looters wandered the beaches, taking pretty much whatever they wanted from unclaimed baggage or corpses.

On August 2, Captain Soto Sanchez and his advance party from the south reached the northernmost camp opposite the wreck of Ubilla's Capitana, the Nuestra Señora de la Regia, at the Bara de Ays (sandbank), two and a half miles south of the present-day Sebastian Inlet. Sanchez immediately reported to Admiral Salmon the loss of his vessel and the general extent of the destruction. Salmon had already moved his people up the beach from the wreck of the Almiranta to take charge of his camp. Despite the commander's suspicions that the fleet's losses had been severe, he was visibly moved by Sanchez's description of the scope of the disaster. But this was no time for emotion; there was considerable work to be done. He knew that to bring all the survivors together in one group was going to aggravate the shortage of rations, but it would also strengthen the defense capabilities of the castaways.

In anticipation of the growing number of people who would soon arrive at the sandbank, the officers tried to make the men enlarge the camp. The whole width of the island from ocean to river would be needed to accommodate everyone. The work went slowly, however, for many were still too weak to accomplish much. A few shelters were built with wreckage hauled up the dunes from the beach; some of the thickets were partially cleared with salvaged boarding cutlasses and lean-tos were constructed and roughly covered with palm fronds or pieces of sail. Clouds of mosquitoes and sand flies plagued the party day and night. The insects were so bad that some of the men buried their wives and children up to their necks in loose sand in an effort to protect them from the perpetual tormentors. Others, notably those who obviously had been accustomed to a more sheltered existence, were almost driven mad by the stinging and biting insects. Smudge fires helped only those few brave enough to crowd closest to the clouds of acrid smoke. There was little choice. One either smothered in smoke or suffered the bites of the pests. Driven by hunger, everyone welcomed the opportunity to forage for food and water.

Although provisions were scarce, there were rabbits, raccoons, opossums, deer, bears and turkeys on the island, which had long been a popular hunting ground for Indians, who frequently came over from the mainland to hunt bear. The fat was rendered from their kills and carried back to their main settlements on the mainland. Since virtually all firearms and shot had been lost at sea, the survivors were limited to the few small animals they could snare, catch by hand or run down. But there was an abundance of fish and shellfish in the waters. Indian River contained many catfish, drum, rays, flounder, mullet, clams, oysters and conches. Piles of refuse shells littered the sandbank, left by generations of Indians who had enjoyed the river's rich bounty. At various times the recalcitrant Ays customarily came there to live and to fish. It was on one of these occasions that the survivors had their first encounter with the Indians.

Admiral Salmon had sent out twenty groups of men to fish for the camp. Having fashioned crude spears from gum saplings, they pursued their quarry into the shallows of the river. And there, quite by accident, the foragers stumbled upon a small fishing party of Ays. The sudden confrontation must have been unsettling to both sides. Early etchings show these Indians with part of their long black hair drawn up into characteristic topknots held in place with slender bone pins while the rest curled around the sides of their heads, so that they seemed to be wearing helmets. Clad in plaited loin belts tied in back with short, arched grass tails, and carrying longbows, with sheaths of bone-tipped arrows slung across their backs, the Indians surely presented a formidable appearance to the Europeans. Despite the Ays' reputation for dispatching an occasional shipwreck victim for whatever goods he might have been fortunate enough to salvage, however, the large number of survivors apparently discouraged, at least for the moment, any similar mischief. Both parties simply withdrew. As uneventful as the encounter was. Admiral Salmon was certainly well aware of his people's precarious position and what the consequences might be if the savages returned in force. Now, more than ever, he must have felt the need to be wary of the unpredictable Ays.

Loaded with treasure the plate fleet of 1715 sailed into history.

Route of the Spanish Plate fleets with x marking loss of the 1715 fleet.

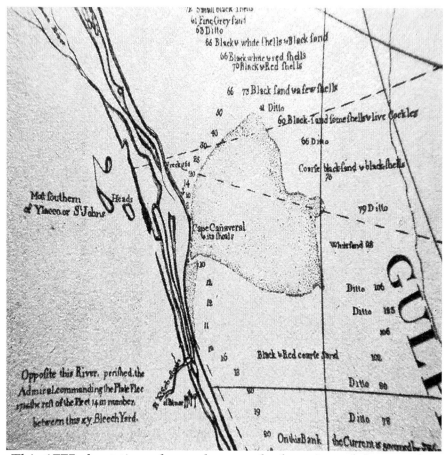

This 1775 chart tipped searchers to the location of the wrecks.

A corroded silver coin can fool you.

Why silver coins are often overlooked.

Pieces of eight on display.

Chapter 6

The Secret Letter

Any hope of help for the castaways would have to come either from St. Augustine about 120 miles to the north, or from Havana, some 360 miles by water to the south. Admiral Salmon knew that he must count on St. Augustine for immediate, temporary assistance; but the main effort would have to come from Havana. It was most important that word be gotten out to these places as quickly as possible.

As soon as the salvaged boats from the Urca and the Nuestra Señora de la Regia reached the main camp, they were immediately made ready to go for help. These were fairly large boats. The launch was about twenty-four feet in length, with a seven-foot beam and a three-foot depth. Each of the boats could be rowed or rigged with lateen sails and could carry up to fifty people. The survivors selected to go on the first boat to St. Augustine were mainly women, children and the most seriously injured, who needed immediate medical attention. There were few of the latter, however, for those who survived the initial ordeal, despite their injuries, died from water inhalation shortly after reaching the beach. The unpleasant task of deciding who would go and who would stay fell to the officers, who now were confronted with another serious problem. Admiral Salmon announced that looters were to return any treasure they had taken to the ships' officers, who would place it under safekeeping, with no questions asked. The offer of amnesty in exchange for their ill-gotten plunder did not impress the looters. Some had collected enough silver and gold from wealthy passengers' luggage to make them rich. And since there were more looters than officers, the former simply disobeyed the commander's order and demanded to be allowed to leave on the boat to St. Augustine. Admiral Salmon refused. The men openly tried bribing some of the subordinate officers for a place on the vessel. When this failed, they attempted to seize one of the launches by force. This might have succeeded but for the quick thinking of an alert lieutenant and a handful of the Capitana's marines armed with several salvaged matchlock muskets.

Finally, as a last resort, the worst of the looters left camp and headed north with their ill-gotten gains. All they had to do, they reasoned, was last until they reached St. Augustine and they would be rich men. Possibly it was the intoxication of new-found wealth in their pockets that numbed them to the fact that they had a 120-mile trek and the wrath of Spanish officialdom ahead of them.

On the morning of August 4, Admiral Salmon took out a leather-bound writing case Captain Lima had rescued from the Urca and carefully composed an open letter to Governor Francisco Corioles at St. Augustine:

Dear Sir:
I have not communicated our mishap to you before because I did not have a vessel at my disposal. I do it now with deep sorrow in my heart since this disaster has been the worst that has occurred in many a year. Not a single ship, whether from the naval escort or from the galleons, has been spared, and because my general Ubilla perished in the Capitana (Flagship), I have taken his place to recover this treasure, which is something of great importance to the service of the King and to the common good. Inasmuch as I am on an island, where we became lost, and we are all so desperately in need of supplies, I am begging you to help me by sending to us as much as you can, or else everyone here will perish. In addition to food supplies, I would like to

receive twenty rifles with their bullets, as much powder as possible, half a dozen axes, another half a dozen shovels and some hoes to remove the sand in order to see whether I can manage to dig out some of the silver and break open part of the hull. His Majesty's treasure and that of private persons, both of which were carried in the hold, sank with the ship in five fathoms of water, in a spot we have duly marked. I am sending my pilot along with this message. I hope and trust that you will help me as soon as possible with some vessels from your garrison. May God grant Your Lordship a long life. August 4, 1715.

Your most humble servant,
Don Francisco Salmon

When he had finished, the admiral wrote a second, secret letter to the governor, which apprised him of the seriousness of their condition.

Dear Sir:
I wish to communicate to you, in confidence, after having sent to you another letter with the pilot, that my men have revolted and are leaving this camp for your garrison heavily loaded with the silver they have stolen. Please, have them arrested and deprived of what they have unlawfully taken. I advise your Lordship that this letter is being carried by the pilot and that on his prompt [return] may depend our ability to remain here watching over His Majesty's treasure and that of private persons, because up to now, nothing has been recovered. I hope our efforts will not be in vain. May God grant Your Lordship a long life. At the Sandbar of Ays. August 4, 1715.

Your most humble servant,
Francisco Salmon

These dispatches were given to Ipilito Sebastian Mendez, pilot of the Nuestra Señora del Carmen, who had been given command of the longboat going to St. Augustine. A few minutes later the select few who were going for help hoisted sail and set out to sea, while those who remained behind called farewells and wished them Godspeed.

Between the 4th and the 10th of August, the two remaining boats were made ready to leave, one of them for St. Augustine. The largest of the three, a launch, was provisioned and loaded with salvaged cargo to sail directly to Havana, Cuba — Spain's most important link with the New World. Admiral Salmon was both anxious to let the outside world know about the fleet's predicament and eager to evacuate from the camp as many nonproductive survivors as possible. Thirty joined Father Francisco de Leon y Cabrera, chaplain of the Nuestra Señora de la Regia, in the second longboat that sailed for St. Augustine on August 7 under the command of Captain Fernando Ignazio Barriga. And the following day, the large launch, commanded by one Captain Perdomo, left for Havana with most of the nobility, the royal officials and other important personages of rank or wealth. One may well imagine that, when this last vessel set sail, the leavetaking was a bit strained. Because of its social standing, one group was exuberantly escaping the deprivations of the castaways' lot while the other was gloomily preparing to embrace it.

As soon as the vessel was dispatched. Admiral Salmon returned to the problem of expanding the main camp at the Barra de Ays for the remaining large population, which now had to establish a more permanent, defensible community there.

Although few cutting tools had been salvaged from the wrecks, work parties began slashing and burning out large clearings in the almost impenetrable thickets of scrub oaks, sea grapes and cabbage palms behind the island's steep sand dunes. Palm- and palmetto- thatched lean-tos were built around the perimeters of these areas, and despite the humid tropical heat, fires were kept burning or smoldering in the middle of the clearings in an attempt to ward off the swarms of mosquitoes and other insects that plagued the castaways. In time, the camp would expand to cover an area over 3,000 feet long, divided into two major camps on the riverside, a network of forty to fifty clearings. Each clearing would hold from ten to fifty and each would be linked to adjoining clearings by tunnel-like trails hacked through the dense undergrowth.

Admiral Salmon had made a wise choice in selecting this site for his main camp. It was a strategic position in case of attack, and it enabled him to keep an eye on the area where the king's treasure had gone down aboard General Ubilla's flagship. The camp could be protected by pickets to the north and south, and since it was on a narrow part of the island, it could not be attacked by surprise from either the river to the west or the ocean to the east. It was the best and most logical choice in the entire area.

While the camp was being enlarged and made more livable, the first longboat of survivors heading for St. Augustine was making good time. The hurricane had cleared the air and the weather was fine, with brisk favorable winds. They covered the 120 miles in three days, arriving at the inlet to St. Augustine on August 7. As the boat rounded the headland and crossed the treacherous sandbars at the mouth of the inlet, the survivors saw in the distance the sloping coquina walls of El Castillo de San Marcos. It was a welcome sight indeed.

When they sailed into the inlet and landed at the quay, a crowd of curious soldiers, settlers and minor officials, informed of their coming by Indian signal fires down the coast, was already there to meet them. Eager hands helped the bedraggled survivors ashore, with particular care for the few women and children, who had especially suffered from the ordeal. Everyone seemed to be speaking at once, questioning, answering, gesturing, gradually learning the terrible news that the combined fleet had been wiped out by the same hurricane that had swept St. Augustine a week before, taking the roofs off many houses and destroying crops, but sparing the settlers the terrible toll of death and destruction it had brought the ships. News of the disaster spread quickly through the town. Crowds grew larger. Boys ran through the streets calling out exaggerated rumors. "All the ships lost! A thousand perish! Few survive!"

Already hard pressed from the deprivations of the recent war and the destruction wrought by the same hurricane that had sunk the fleet, St. Augustine citizens shared what few comforts they had with the survivors. The injured were immediately taken to homes and cared for, clothing was found for those who needed it, and everyone was fed — with the first decent food they had eaten in over a week.

Accompanied by crowds of curious people, Ipilito Sebastian and the other representatives of the fleet were escorted down the narrow, crooked streets, past rows of whitewashed coquina-rock houses, directly to the governor's residence. The house was a large, sturdy two-story structure well designed for the Florida climate. A wide, covered second-story balcony occupied a large part of the front. There was no chimney, nor were there glass windows. Instead, a projecting frame of wood rails covered the windows. On the northwest side of the house, there was a lookout tower surmounted by a flagstaff bearing the royal flag.

When Governor Corioles read the dispatches from Admiral Salmon, he immediately started the official machinery that would hasten relief to the people at the Barra de Ays. His first act was to write a formal statement to the king summarizing the recent events. In this document, dated August 7 and signed before Juan Solana, the court clerk, the governor reported that a longboat had arrived carrying two letters from Admiral Salmon dated August 4. From these he learned that the commander of the Flota portion of the fleet. General Ubilla, had gone down with his flagship, and that in order to recover the king's treasure, which was in the hull of this vessel at a depth of five fathoms in the spot knows as "El Palmar de Ays," located forty leagues to the south of the garrison. Admiral Salmon had requested immediate help in the form of food and other supplies. "Steps are being taken," said the governor, "to send this help by repairing the longboat and dispatching other vessels." He added that very little could be sent, however, since there had been a long drought and, consequently, a crop failure, besides the damage done by the storm. He said that he had issued the necessary orders to secure depositions from the pilot and other survivors and learn exactly what had taken place.

Next, to prevent St. Augustinians from going after the treasure, the governor issued a decree forbidding all persons to leave St. Augustine to travel either north or south, unless they had special permits. He ordered everyone who owned a vessel—a pirogue, a canoe or a flat-bottomed boat—to bring it to the main Guard House within six hours. Failure to comply could mean a fine and imprisonment. This decree, also signed on August 7, was designed to keep looters away from the site until official salvage operations could be put into effect.

Following this, Governor Corioles issued a proclamation, announced by the beating of war drums through the town, asking the royal treasurer to "open the warehouse containing maize and corn meal in order to help the survivors of the wreck." The royal treasurer reluctantly complied, but emphasized that the amount of stores in the warehouse was "hardly enough to attend to the needs of the garrison."

A sworn statement was then taken from Captain Sebastian Mendez, pilot of General Ubilla's flagship, the Nuestra Señora del Carmen, which outlined the events from the time the fleet left Cuba until it was lost in the hurricane on the Florida coast.

Finally, Governor Corioles met with Francisco Melendez Marques, the royal auditor, and Salvador Garcia de Villegas, the royal treasurer and acting chief of supplies. It was agreed that food and supplies would be sent to the survivors despite the shortage in the garrison; a large sloop and several pirogues would be dispatched as soon as possible. After arriving at the camp, the sloop would be used to search for the remains of the wreck containing the king's treasure. Further, in support of the admiral's request, it was decided that the royal auditor should go to the watch post on the Sand Bar of Matanzas to instruct the officer in charge to intercept looters coming up the beach and to confiscate stolen goods. The auditor was to see that those items for which the beach-walkers lacked proof of ownership were collected and sent back to the royal treasury in St. Augustine.

The following day, August 8, the governor wrote Admiral Salmon the letter that was to accompany the relief party to the Barra de Ays:

Dear Sir:

I received your two letters of the fourth with a feeling of sorrow and regret, which I now share with Your Lordship, for the deplorable misfortune represented by the loss of the two fleets, the navy ships and the galleons, a very severe blow to the Monarchy, since His Majesty, to whom may God, Our Lord, grant a long life, must be awaiting the arrival of these treasures to help ease some of the heavy burdens of the Crown. Since these are things that occur because of decisions from Above, we as Catholics have nothing left to do but to accept the Divine Will, which is what we ask Him for every day in our prayers.

For the past three years, this garrison has suffered under grave hardships, both because of the belated arrival of the provisions from New Spain and because of the general drought that, having lasted for that period of time, did not allow us even to collect seeds. In addition to this, the latest hurricane, which caused such havoc in the fleets, destroyed and ruined all the plantations, as the men you have sent here will testify when they return.

The longboat, which arrived yesterday, will leave today

carrying the provisions and supplies that Your Lordship requested; I hope you will understand that this is all we can send at the present time. Since we do not have any firelocks, none are included in the shipment; neither are there muskets or arquebuses, because your emissary refused them on the grounds that they were of no use to him. In regard to vessels, the Royal Officials and myself have agreed to send the large bilander [a small two-masted sailboat], inasmuch as the other is rotten and, therefore, entirely useless. We have begun to caulk the large one, and the shipwrights have taken out six boards. Others are being looked for to replace them, but even if they should be found, God only knows whether or not there will be an artisan to put them in place, because I do not have masters or workmen in any field, my repeated requests to have some sent from Havana or New Spain having come to naught.

His Majesty's treasure may be brought up a river and eight leagues over land — thus without having to go out into the ocean — to this garrison. This task can be accomplished little by little, it being my duty as governor to apprise you of all this, with the warning that in the months from August to October the side winds and hurricanes are frequent in these shores. I do not doubt, therefore, that, as in the past. Your Lordship will now show the same understanding and experience, together with the evident zeal to do what is best for the royal service, and will, therefore, adopt the safest course, because the risks involved in taking the treasure to Havana at this time and hence to Spain are too great. I cannot avoid to remind Your Lordship of all these things because, having thus done my duty, nobody will be able in the future to level any charges or claims against me. On the other hand, I hereby offer all the help that I or this garrison can give in the way of pirogues, people acquainted with the rivers and swamps, and anything else needed for the recovery and safety of the royal treasure, as it is my duty to do. I am well aware of the meagerness of the provisions I am sending and of those I will be able to send—they amount to almost nothing considering the large number of victims.

But I must limit myself because of the shortage we now face and the pressing needs of the garrison. Since everything comes from abroad, there being no resources here, I must be careful now and until such a time as the situado (a support dole) arrives, specially in the months ahead, which are dangerous to navigation in this coast, as I have already stated.

So that if the situado is lost—God forbid!—or is late, it will be necessary (to avoid dismantling the garrison) to resort to the strictest rationing, as I had to do in the past, when in desperation the infantry and inhabitants of this garrison had to eat horses, dogs and cats in March and April of the year 1712.

The bilander will leave as soon as it is ready, and I am doing all I can to have it repaired in the shortest possible time. In it, I will send you all the provisions that our circumstances permit. I regret not to have the means at the moment to extend any other help to Your Lordship; but, as you know, I had to hastily send the longboat to you today and, as I have already stated, we are lacking in almost everything here. I am very sorry about the death of General Ubilla and the other victims. May God, Our Lord, grant them peace and rest, and to you a long life.

Florida, August 8, 1715.

Your most humble servant,
Don Francisco de Corioles y Martinez
To: The Admiral Francisco Salmon

The same day the governor wrote to Admiral Salmon, Melendez, the royal auditor, left by boat for the watchtower at Matanzas Inlet, sixteen miles south of the settlement. This outpost guarded the city's southern water access to the sea. The inlet was a natural barrier to anyone moving north up the coast.

When Melendez reached the outpost at sunrise, Friday, August 10, he found that a number of the survivors from the wrecks were on the south side of the inlet, where a petty officer, Luis Rodrigo, and his guard at the watchtower had kept them until he arrived. Melendez and the soldiers took boats across the river and immediately searched the party. In a letter written to Governor Corioles the same day, the auditor reported that he had collected four hundred pesos from the looters. In addition, he requested the return of a canoe "in view of the fact that the survivors can hardly walk because of sore feet, so that some of them are unable to walk overland to the garrison"; and additional food supplies, "hardtack and fifty pounds of corn, because I had to distribute the quantity I brought with me among the survivors."

In his letter of reply, which returned with the requested canoe and supplies, the governor ordered Melendez to proceed as soon as he could to Admiral Salmon's camp and inspect the hulls that contained the registered treasure. Once he had appraised the situation, he was to return immediately to St. Augustine and report to the governor. Before Melendez could leave the watchtower for the survivors' camp, however, he was approached by Father Manuel de Quinones, Notary Public of the Ecclesiastical Court, who asked by what authority he was there. Melendez replied that certainly the Father knew that he was there by virtue of the governor's decree in response to Admiral Salmon's request that the looters be intercepted and relieved of stolen goods.

Father Quinones admitted that he was aware of the decree and that he understood the survivors had opened all the cases and taken out all the silver and gold they contained. Therefore, he said, it was the duty of representatives of the Church to see that all recovered goods be turned over to the Commissary of the Holy Crusade at St. Augustine. Furthermore, anyone who dared interfere with the Church's wishes, including the governor, was subject to excommunication.

Melendez quite obviously had no wish to oppose the strong authority of the Spanish Church in this serious matter. Avoiding the issue by following the governor's order, he left at once for the camp at the Barra de Ays.

Meanwhile, the first help from St. Augustine arrived at the survivors' camp in the form of small boats and canoes with food, tools and, most important, a number of Indian militia composed of Yamassee, Guali and refugee Apalachees, dispatched by the governor to help the castaways by foraging for food. Needless to say, their arrival created considerable excitement among the stranded people. It represented their first glimmer of hope since the disaster. The relief party also reported the good news that it had passed Father de Leon and the second boatload of survivors that was making its way to St. Augustine.

Conditions on the Barra de Ays had gradually improved, largely through the efforts to make more substantial shelters in the clearings. What had been insufferable hardship soon became routine. Still, everyone was forced to remain on extremely short rations.

Not long after the boats had departed for St. Augustine and Havana, Ays Indians visited the island. They apparently came in peace in spite of their fierce reputation, and Admiral Salmon encouraged them to supply the camp with fresh fish and game in exchange for trinkets and other trade items. Although the fifteen hundred or so survivors surely could have held out against all the Ays in existence, living along the coast between Cape Canaveral and Jupiter Inlet, the commander undoubtedly knew that these Indians could be trusted only as long as they believed that any trouble they caused would bring certain retribution from the Spanish garrison. Without this veiled threat, however, and perhaps even with it, Admiral Salmon had no way of knowing how long the Indians would remain peaceful.

As the camp grew larger and better organized, one of the first necessities was to find a better source of drinking water.

The river was brackish, and there were no springs or creeks on the island. It had not taken much investigation by the more knowledgeable officers to discover that the sloping west bank of the sandbar was satisfactory for building Spanish surface wells. Although the departure of the boats had reduced the camp's population by about a hundred, the number of wells would have to be increased to fill the needs of the remaining fourteen hundred. This job was undertaken by several groups of men who would concentrate the building of wells on the points extending into the river, as close as possible to various main camp clearings. The size of the wells depended upon how many people they needed to accommodate and the amount of building material available. Smaller wells were no larger than barrels, and their construction was simple. A hole was dug down through the soft sand to the water table, which on the west side of the island was never more than four feet below the surface. Loose sand and dirt were scooped out until the hole was large enough to allow a good seepage of water. A barrel with its top and bottom knocked out was then set halfway down into the water-filled hole to prevent the sides from caving in. Sand was filled around the outside of the barrel up to its rim, creating in effect a small reservoir into which water trickled and could be dipped out.

Larger wells required more work, but the method was just as simple. Once a hole was dug and cleared, salvaged ship timbers and parts of cargo cases were dragged up from the beach and placed one atop another around the sides of the hole to form a box. Both inside and out, the timbers were shored with short segments of hickory or sea-grape poles. Sand was then packed around the exterior to make a box-shaped well so substantial that modern archaeologists found several of them intact at the campsite almost 250 years later. The survivors probably needed about twelve such wells.

With the axes, tools, muskets and food from the first relief party from St. Augustine, rapid improvements were made in the camp.

The Indians quickly eased the crowded conditions in many of the clearings by constructing numerous thatched huts. They also hunted and fished for the survivors, teaching them how to sun-dry and smoke meat for preservation and how to prepare and eat sea grapes, palmetto berries, and the hearts of cabbage palms for nourishment.

Although Melendez, the royal auditor, was the first outside official to visit the site and dispassionately appraise what was happening, the fleets' officers were not overly enthusiastic in welcoming him. Admiral Salmon was more concerned when he read Governor Corioles's dispatch suggesting that he deliver the king's treasure to St. Augustine. His concern grew when Melendez told him of the Church's demand that it all be turned over to the Royal Commissary of the Crusade unless one wished to risk the punishment of excommunication. The commander told Melendez that he and the trade agents represented by General Echeverz had already decided that it would be inadvisable to send the treasure to St. Augustine and that when it was recovered, it should be sent directly to Havana. To absolve the royal auditor of any blame, Admiral Salmon and the trade agents spelled out their intentions in an affidavit, which they signed.

Melendez stayed at camp only long enough to note that nothing had yet been done about salvaging any of the treasure; then he left for St. Augustine to turn over the confiscated valuables to the Commissary of the Crusade. Throughout that day the church bells of St. Augustine tolled and edicts were published threatening to excommunicate anyone who interfered with the Commissary's efforts to collect the stolen goods. By then the Commissary had instructed Governor Corioles to order the officer at the watchtower of Matanzas to cooperate fully with their representative. Captain Sebastian Lopez de Toledo, who had taken over the royal auditor's job of collecting plunder from the stragglers stopped at the inlet.

While these things were taking place in Florida, other

events were occurring in Cuba that would soon sharply alter the fate of the castaways at the Barra de Ays. At 2 A.M. on August 15, the first survivors of the disaster reached Havana in the large launch. Despite the hour, Governor Casatores was awakened immediately and told the news. In disbelief he read Admiral Salmon's letter explaining what had happened. Then, dressing hurriedly, the governor asked that Captain Perdomo and other officials in the party meet with him at once so that he could learn the details and determine what must be done.

The weary survivors told him that there were about 1,400 men, women and children stranded on the Barra de Ays with little food and water, but that some help had probably already arrived from St. Augustine. When the governor asked if any of the king's treasure had been saved, all they could tell him was that two of the ships had been lost close to shore but nothing had yet been recovered.

Not long after daybreak, news of the disaster spread through Havana. The citizens were appalled by the great loss. Cathedral bells tolled the message long and mournfully throughout the day. Meanwhile, Governor Casatores did what he could to cope with the situation. After meeting with his government officials, he ordered the Sergeant Major of Havana, Don Juan de Hoyo Solorzano, to find and provision vessels at once to sail for the Barra de Ays to assist in the rescue, equipping some of the ships for lengthy salvage operations. He wrote the king two letters notifying him of the loss. These were dispatched the same day, along with some of the more prominent survivors aboard the frigate Francisco, which was about to sail for Rochelle, France. Although Phillip V would not learn of the disaster until September 7 when the letters would reach him. Governor Casatores knew the king would expect him to act with the utmost speed. And this he did, as far as the conditions of the time permitted. Seven ships were found, provisioned and made ready for sea in a remarkably short time—no simple task, considering that some of the vessels were to remain on the Florida coast for an indefinite time. Thirty experienced divers were enlisted. Most were Indians from the coast of South America; the best of these were ex-pearl divers from the Island of Margarita. These men were eager to go, knowing that for each chest of silver they recovered they would be well paid. All they would be expected to give in return was a full day's work under water from sunup until sundown seven days a week for the next few months. And to facilitate that task, special salvage equipment had been loaded aboard the ships: quantities of hemp and chain, grappling hooks, baskets, dredges, long-handled rakes, diving bells, empty chests and all the other necessities required for a prolonged salvage effort. Finally, the ships cleared from Havana and followed the fleet's route northward. Guided by several officers and returning crew members, the vessels reached the Barra de Ays on September 10, 1715, anchoring a safe distance offshore from Admiral Salmon's camp.

It was a happy day for the remaining survivors. Boatloads of food, water and supplies were landed immediately to ease their need. In the following days a steady stream of cutters and longboats began transferring survivors to the rescue vessels. As each was loaded, it departed, either going to St. Augustine or returning to Havana, where passage could be arranged for the people going on to Spain. Then the fleet's officers and crews were removed to Havana and their depositions taken in an effort to determine the details of the disaster.

At long last the ordeal of the castaways was over.

Chapter 7

Of Pirates and Salvagers

The Spanish quickly prepared to recover the treasure lost with the 1715 fleet. Although Hoyo Solorzano was in charge of the salvage operation, the man in charge of diving was a veteran named Clemente, whose first responsibility was to the king's treasure. The salvagers knew the location of General Ubilla's Capitana, and they soon searched for and found the remains of his Almiranta. These two ships had carried the bulk of the royal and private treasure and were therefore the salvagers' primary targets. But locating the wrecks and finding the treasure were two different things. Clemente knew that when some of the ships struck, their hulls were ripped open and cargo strewn over a wide area, while the wreckage came to rest elsewhere. In some instances, hulls and decks had completely separated, the bottoms winding up in one place and the upper works, if they had not disintegrated, in another. To complicate matters further, it was the time of year when salvage conditions on this particular coast were at their absolute worst. Strong northeast winds kept echelons of cold, slate-gray Atlantic waves rolling over the wrecks and thundering ashore relentlessly. With the very best conditions, underwater visibility was little more than an arm's length, but now Clemente's divers would be lucky to see their hands twelve inches in front of their faces. Nor could the large salvage ships be brought in over the wrecks. The salvagers would have to work from the longboats and cutters. These vessels, capable of carrying thirty to forty men each, were more maneuverable and less likely to get into serious trouble in the tumbling surf.

Pry bars, rakes, ropes, baskets and grappling hooks were loaded aboard the boats, and the men started searching for the Capitana's treasure. While some of the boats concentrated their efforts on the main part of the wreck, others dragged light grappling irons back and forth along the course Clemente estimated the ship had taken coming in.

Sharp-eyed helmsmen stood at the tillers ready to angle the boats into particularly large waves. The Indians bent to their oars, and the hooks bit easily through the soft white bottom sand. If the hooks snagged rocks, the boats were backed down until the obstacles were disengaged. Then the procedure was repeated as the vessels gradually moved into deeper water. Clemente's boat was two hundred yards from shore, working between two broad ridges of shell-rock outcroppings, when the hooks grabbed solidly, then came up with fragments of oak on their tines. The cutter dropped anchor immediately, and divers were sent down to investigate. Minutes later Clemente had the news. The hooks had struck the shattered under-hull of the flagship. Collision with the bottom had sheared it off at the turn of the bilge. The weight of the ballast rock and tons of silver loaded on the orlop deck had sent it straight to the bottom the moment it separated from the upper works. With any kind of luck, the divers should find most of the treasure intact, stacked on the very timbers that had supported it aboard ship.

Clemente signaled nearby boats to assist him, then dove down himself to evaluate the situation. As best he could tell, the hulk lay in a sand valley between outcroppings of limestone, but the diving engineer could hardly stay with the wreck. Visibility was close to zero. The surge threw him in one direction and the strong offshore current whipped him in another. Three times he was forced to surface for air before he had any idea of how the cargo lay in the cold, swirling blue-gray world below. But finally he felt the chests; some were still stacked in precise rows, whereas others lay buried or broken amid the complex jumble of broken timbers, tangled cordage and scattered ballast rock.

When Clemente finally came out of the water, he was not pleased with the prospects. It was the time of year when there would be no calming of seas, no hope of the water's clearing. The coast would be punished by unrelenting winds and waves throughout the fall and winter, with no real letup until the following summer. If the boats were to be effective, they would have to remain over the wrecks, rolling and pitching in the surf while the heavy chests were being fished up from the bottom. And no man knew better than he what his divers could expect, working blind and fighting the currents, the numbing cold, the quick fatigue, the fatal exhaustion.

Despite Clemente's apprehensions, his divers must have been eager to go. Now that only four fathoms separated them from their goal, the attraction had to have been overpowering. Perhaps Clemente saw it on their faces, the mixture of eagerness and fear flashing momentarily across their dark features each time the wave-tossed cutter tilted dangerously close to capsizing. But as quickly as danger passed, they would have thought only of the rich reward that lay almost within their grasp. Each man would receive a percentage of what he found and Clemente knew that before this was over they would have earned it. Naked, they stood waiting at the gunwale. Clemente nodded and they plunged over.

On the bottom the Indians fought their way through the blue murk, towing the long hemp ropes behind them. Each time the surge swept shoreward, they dung like leeches to the nearest rock ledge or broken timber. When the rushing wall of water passed they thrashed forward, scrambling through the wreck's debris, grabbing onto chests of silver, then fumbling to untie the ropes around their waists while the new surge swept in, lifting and twisting their bodies in its cold embrace. Two minutes passed into three as numbed fingers knotted the ropes securely to chest handles. Then with the air hunger finally growing to a sharp, insistent pain, they started up the ropes hand over hand, exhaling a steady stream of bubbles from their bursting lungs.

In the cutter, as in the other longboats that had converged over the wreckage, men strained at the lines in their effort to haul the chests up, almost capsizing the craft. At length the first chests emerged and were with difficulty hoisted aboard. Many more followed. The divers were flushed with their first success, but it was to be short lived.

Three hours later the wind freshened and began shifting directions erratically. It gusted from all points of the compass until the boats were pitching and rolling wildly in the welter of colliding waves. Finally, Clemente saw that it was useless to remain where they were. Several boats had already dragged anchors and were in danger of being swept into the same oblivion that had claimed the fleet. Reluctantly he ordered his divers up and back to the ships.

For the next five days the steepening gray seas were whipped into a fury by a succession of northers. A safe distance at sea, the salvage fleet rode them out on double bow and stern anchors. Even when the winds finally abated, there was no noticeable change in the rampaging foam-crested hillocks of water that thundered through the surf to crash onto the narrow, weed-strewn beach at the foot of the dunes.

Only after the winds shifted to the south did the waves slowly subside, and on the eighth day Clemente's crews returned to the wrecks.

Now their difficulties were compounded. The water was as opaque as pea soup. The wreckage and the silver were still there, but the storm seas had done their dirty work. Many of the chests were buried under six inches of sand. What could not be seen had to be felt for and then dug out with bare hands and crowbars. The divers went to work with less enthusiasm than before. Although the Indians were accustomed to hardships, the rigors of diving under these conditions soon sapped their strength. Few could stay underwater more than three minutes before having to surface for air. In those brief moments on the bottom, they wasted precious time and energy simply struggling to keep from being washed away while they blindly dug and tugged to free half-buried chests from the sand so that they could be recovered. Sometimes while the chests were being hauled to the surface, ropes slipped and the prize plummeted back to the bottom again. Clemente faithfully noted in his records that in the first week of salvage he lost three men. Two were crushed by falling chests and a third expired in what the salvage master termed an "unfortunate incident." He was devoured by a shark. Still, Clemente drove the men hard, scrupulously recording that despite losses he was getting results, recovering many chests of the king's treasure. In the following weeks, both the returns and the divers' mortality rate climbed. Clemente was getting results, at a price.

The divers working on the Almiranta were confronted with similar hardships. The vessel was relatively intact, but the treasure was not easily accessible. The men worked in such shallow water that each time a wave lifted a longboat on its crest, then dropped it into its trough, the salvage vessel was precariously close to crushing its bottom on the upthrust wreckage of the sunken ship. The first things the divers recovered were the valuable brass swivel guns mounted on the warship's gunwales. Then they began dismantling the wreckage so that they could gain easy entry to the hold, using iron bars to pry loose deck planking. If a diver surfaced and said he believed there were chests buried under a segment of hull, the big grappling hook went into service. It was a five-foot-long heavy iron implement with four to six tines angling up from one end like boughs on an inverted Christmas tree. The hook was dropped overboard, and divers positioned it in the wreckage. A line was run from the grappling hook to the capstan of the nearest ship, which hauled it in until the hull section was moved. These hooks were also used to tear up decks or to pull hulls apart when it was necessary for the divers to get inside without too great a risk to life or limb. At least one of the hooks was lost by the salvagers and lay undiscovered on the shifting sand bottom for the next 250 years.

The necessity of having the larger ships in close to shore, where the capstans could be utilized for pulling apart the wrecks, petrified the Spanish. A shift of wind or current could swing the big salvage vessels onto one of the wrecks and cause damage they could ill afford.

After several weeks of intensive work, the salvagers had accumulated a large amount of silver. The coins were originally packed in cloth sacks inside wooden chests. As soon as possible the chests had to be opened, the sacks removed and the silver washed carefully in fresh water to prevent corrosion. This was done at Admiral Salmon's camp on shore. After the silver had been washed, it was repacked in clean bags and put into dry chests, which had been brought for that purpose. Clemente ordered a small storehouse built on the west side of the island, where the salvaged treasure was kept under armed guard. Despite every precaution to prevent divers from pilfering coins, such pilfering undoubtedly occurred, not only among the Indians but among some of the Spaniards as well. The opportunity was there, and the best Clemente could do was make it as unattractive as possible. Anyone caught with treasure not belonging to him was promptly executed. Pilfering, however, was the least of his worries.

News of the disaster had traveled quickly through the Caribbean. In such places as the Bahamas, Barbados and Jamaica, people listened with more than casual interest when they learned that an entire treasure fleet had foundered on the Florida east coast and that a small band of Spanish salvagers was even then fishing up enormous sums of silver and gold. To many seafaring scallywags the particularly appealing part was all that wealth lying there virtually unprotected, a prize for anyone willing to go after it. Clemente anticipated trouble.

The question in his mind was, "When?"

The king of England was kept well apprised of the loss of the Spanish vessels by intelligence reports from the New World. Governor Spotswood of Virginia wrote to the Crown: "There is advice of considerable events in these parts that the Spanish Plate Fleet, richly laden, consisting of eleven sail, are, except one, lately cast away in the Gulf of Florida to the southward of St. Augustine and that a barkalonga [an open 50 foot single-masted sailing vessel] sent from the Havana to fetch off from the continent some passengers of distinction who were in that fleet, having recovered from the wrecks a considerable quality of plate, is likewise cast away about forty miles to the northward of St. Augustine. I think it my duty to inform his Majesty of this accident which may be improved to the advantage of his Majesty's subjects by encouraging them to attempt the recovery of some of that immense wealth."

Few Englishmen in the colonies needed any official encouragement to tweak the beard of the Spanish king whenever such an opportunity arose. On November 21, 1715, Governor Archibald Hamilton of Jamaica commissioned two ships, the Eagle, commanded by Captain Edward James, and the Bathsheba, commanded by Captain Henry Jennings, to go to sea for six months to hunt pirates. But Jennings, a successful privateer from the recent war, had other plans. Instead of suppressing piracy, he intended doing a little pirating of his own. Furthermore, Lord Hamilton was undoubtedly aware of Jennings's scheme, and it was later widely believed that he had been its architect.

In any event, history relates that Jennings's fleet of two ships and three sloops, outfitted in Jamaica and Barbados, sailed directly to the site of the Spanish salvage camp on the Florida east coast and landed three hundred men. The raiders drove off two commissaries and the sixty soldiers guarding the storehouse, seized the accumulated treasure and headed back toward Jamaica. On the way they met a Spanish ship bound from Porto Bello to Havana with a rich cargo, including bales of cochineal, casks of indigo and 60,000 pieces of eight. After plundering the vessel, Jennings let her go. The rovers repaired to Jamaica with their plunder and divided some 120,000 pieces of eight among all concerned.

Clemente returned to his salvage duties, driving his divers all the harder and gradually accumulating more treasure in the storehouse on the beach. Periodically, salvage vessels carried the wealth to Havana. Some of the ships made the crossing without mishap; others, however, fell into the hands of raiders. Jennings meanwhile waited for the Spanish at the Barra de Ays to stockpile a goodly amount of treasure before he deemed it profitable enough to make a second attempt. Finally, on January 26, 1716, two months after his first successful raid on the Spanish camp, he struck again. This time he sailed to the Florida coast in the Bathsheba, dropped anchor offshore and waited until night to land his men. The next morning the force moved on the camp with drawn arms. Clemente looked at their weapons and asked if England and Spain had resumed the war. Jennings said no, that he and his men had come to fish on the wrecks. Clemente replied that the wrecks belonged to the king of Spain and that he and his people were trying to find the lost treasure. But Jennings was obviously in no mood to quibble over who owned the valuable property, especially since he had the salvagers at a disadvantage. Hoping perhaps that he could buy them off, Clemente offered the raiders 25,000 pieces of eight to leave the wrecks and the salvagers alone. Jennings responded by taking the 25,000 and all the rest of the silver in the storehouse. He also stripped the salvagers of their valuables, helped himself to four small cannon, two of which were brass, and plugged the muzzles of two others left behind. Again the pirates made a clean getaway with their plunder, which according to the Spanish amounted to some 120,000 pieces of eight and wrought silver, though others said it amounted to far more.

Havana responded to this final indignity by sending Don Juan Francisco de Vale to complain to the governor of Jamaica.

Lord Hamilton's probable response was to commission another ship or two to go forth and "suppress" the freebooters. But Havana's emissary was no fool. He recalled that when the Spanish captured an English vessel on the coast near Porto Bello because it was trading where foreigners were not allowed to trade, the English captain had told him that the governor owned a fourth part of the English raider. Vale said he had also heard it mentioned openly by gentlemen in Jamaica that the governor was part owner of all vessels sent to prey on the Spanish camp. Later he reported that he had traced some of the stolen wealth to the governor's house.

Despite this seemingly continual involvement in such matters, however, Jamaica's Lord Hamilton was by no means the only instigator of the frequent depredations on the Spanish salvage fleet on the Florida coast. Jennings's successes simply opened the door wider to greater excesses. As an example of the busy intrigues in the English colonial island communities, witness the deposition of one John Vickers of the island of Providence:

In November last, Benjamin Hornigold [an infamous pirate who once served under Blackbeard] arrived in Providence in the sloop Mary of Jamaica belonging to Augustine Golding which Hornigold took upon the Spanish coast. Soon after taking it he took a Spanish sloop loaded with dry goods and sugar, which cargo he disposed of at Providence. But the Spanish sloop was taken from him by Captain Jennings of the sloop Bathsheba of Jamaica. In January, Hornigold left Providence in said sloop Mary, having on board 140 men, six guns and eight pattereros [small breechloading cannons] and soon after returning with another Spanish sloop from the Florida coast. After he fitted out said sloop at Providence he sent Golding's sloop back to Jamaica to be returned to the owners and in March last sailed to Providence in the Spanish sloop, having on board 200 men but bound on a secret mission.

Somehow, despite the depredations of the English pirates,

Clemente's men managed to salvage about 80 percent of the lost treasure during their first major salvage effort from September 1715 to the middle of April 1716, when the operation temporarily ended. Governor Corioles, who had been supplying the Spanish salvagers from St. Augustine, was notified by officers at the Barra de Ay that further assistance was no longer necessary, that he need not send the Indians that he had intended since there would be sufficient personnel arriving with the Spanish fleet from Havana to load the treasure. Further, they did not think that the returns of salvaging on the wrecks would pay for the cost of maintaining themselves any longer on the Florida coast, and they were therefore withdrawing to Havana.

On June 11, 1716, the governor of Havana, the salvage officers and the royal officials of Cuba held a meeting to determine how best to transport the salvaged treasure back to Spain. They decided to divide the risks between two ships, the 60-gun Nuestra Señora del Carmen and the 44-gun Principe de Asturias. Since the Carmen was the more heavily armed of the two, she would carry two-thirds of the treasure; the remaining one-third would go on the Principe. At another meeting, officials and shipmasters ratified the decision. Loaded aboard the Carmen for the royal account were: 680,697 pesos in silver coins packed in 227 cedarwood chests; 152,428 pesos 7 reales in 181 silver bars in 37 chests; 16,000 pesos in 1,000 doubloons of 8 escudos, Mexican serrated. Total; 849,125 pesos 7 reales. The grand total for the king on the two vessels amounted to: 1,273,688 pesos 7 reales. The fact that this much treasure was being returned to Spain indicated not only how effective the first Spanish salvage effort had been, but also that despite a shortage from pirating, Havana had made up the difference from its own coffers so that the king's share would be complete. The two ships carrying the treasure to Spain crossed the Atlantic without mishap and arrived at Cadiz on August 25, 1716, four years after the Flota and the Galeones had set out to get it from the New World.

Most of the private and unregistered treasure was still missing.

As soon as the Spanish left the salvage site, the English swarmed in to "fish" on the wrecks. Most of the vessels were probably from New Providence in the Bahamas; others were from Jamaica and the Carolinas. Some idea of how the English responded to news of the Spanish pull-out is indicated in a letter about the situation in Jamaica written to a Mr. Burchett on May 13, 1716, by a Captain Belchin of H.M.S. Diamond: "There have been at least twenty sloops fitted for the wrecks and if I had stayed [in Jamaica] a week longer I do not believe I should have kept enough men to bring the ship home. I lost ten in two days before I sailed, being all mad to go a-wrecking as they put it."

Not one to miss such an opportunity. Captain Henry Jennings returned again to the scene of his former triumphs, this time acting as guard and overseer of the operations as stated in a document of April 22, 1716: "Captain Jennings arrived at Providence and brought in a prize of a French ship mounting 32 guns which he had taken in the Bay of Hounds, carrying a very rich cargo of European goods for the Spanish trade. He then went in said ship to the wrecks where he served as commodore and guard ship."

On June 3, 1716, Governor Spotswood of Virginia complained to the Council of Trade that pirates were taking over complete control of the Bahamas. He committed to prison one Captain Forbes for beating the Spanish from their batteries on the Florida coast while they were guarding the wrecks, and because he was also an accessory to the taking of a French ship. But the temptation to join in the illicit salvaging was apparently too great even for Governor Spotswood, who on June 15,1716, ordered Captain Harry Beverly, commander of the sloop Virgin of Virginia, to go to the wrecks to fish up what he could. And in another document from Jamaica we read: "It is evident that under the pretext of a report that there were pirates on the coast of America, there fitted out in

Jamaica fourteen sloops manned by 3,000 men to clear those seas. But the remedy was worse than the disease." The entry describes how one sloop commanded by "a tawny Moor named Fernando Fernandez" openly practiced piracy, the commander giving as his excuse that he was under orders from the governor of Jamaica. "The English plunder under the pretext of clearing the coasts of pirates," continues the entry, "[but] against all equity [they] have been diving for the silver which was lost on the Flota at Palmar." Thus the English helped themselves to the Spanish wrecks from early 1716 until early 1718, when the Spanish decided to launch another salvage attempt on the wrecks they had not officially abandoned.

On arriving at the Palmar de Ays, the Spanish found the English firmly ensconced there. The trespassers had already erected some dwellings and were proceeding to create a fortified town surrounded by earthwork and fascines, with four cannon. The Spanish opened fire immediately, killing one and wounding several others, but they were no match for the superior number of English. Eventually they yielded and returned to Cuba. On learning what had happened, the governor of Havana urged citizens to finance a new and more powerful expeditionary force to drive out the English. This they did, mustering a sufficient number of men and ships to return to Florida and make short work of the intruders at the Palmar de Ays. According to a Spanish account, "On September 18, 1718, the new expeditionary force returned to Havana with the following prizes: five excellent bilanders [sloop-rigged sailing vessels], 98 Negro slaves, 86 British prisoners, 80 pesos in coins and wrought silver and other things of less importance. Before they could be arrested, more than 60 of the British managed to get away in canoes. Twenty escaped later to the island of Providence after they overpowered a Spanish crew of six on the vessel in which they were being taken to Havana. But our expedition left a garrison of 140 men to the defense of the post, provisioning them with supplies that had been wrested from the English; and four of our vessels with which to continue the diving operations."

This was the Spaniards' last big salvage effort on the wrecks. It is doubtful that they recovered very much, because the first attempt had claimed most of the treasure. Two years after the loss, the wrecks were broken up and scattered; most of the material sank into the sandy bottom and was lost. What little had not been salvaged by the Spanish the first time had certainly been picked over extensively by the English. The second attempt continued through the summer and fall and terminated sometime in 1719, followed by gradually diminished fishing for treasure from passers- by until the locations of the wrecks began to fade from man's memory.

Interestingly, the notorious Captain Henry Jennings never paid for his crimes of piracy. When Captain Woodes Rogers, renowned among other things for having captured one of the Manila galleons, became governor of the Bahamas Islands, he posted a royal proclamation dated September 5, 1717, pardoning all pirates who would surrender before September 5, 1718. Jennings wisely turned himself in and never again returned to his nefarious career as a freebooter. Instead, the ex-pirate retired to Bermuda and lived out his life as a respected gentleman of means — a life made all the more bearable, perhaps, by an ample supply of Spanish silver.

Chapter 8

Romans's Clue

After the last Spanish salvage effort, all evidence of what had happened to the Spanish Plate Fleet of 1715 gradually disappeared into the musty pigeon-holes of time. Survivors of the drama lived out their lives and died. Carefully kept Spanish records were filed away and forgotten. Legions of hungry teredo worms consumed every exposed piece of wooden wreckage, and the shifting sands of the Atlantic buried the rest. On the Barra de Ays, nature's reclamation of the old Spanish salvage camp and the camp of the English was equally swift. Wood structures and palm-thatched roofs crumbled to dust. The man-made scars were healed with new vegetation, and the earth claimed all that remained.

Half a century after the disaster almost everything was gone, but the incident was not quite forgotten. In the late 1760s, English cartographer Bernard Romans passed through the area and was obviously well aware of what had occurred there, despite inaccuracies in some of his facts. Later, he described the event in his book, A Concise Natural History of East and West Florida, published in 1775. On page 273, Romans details the topographical aspects of the Indian River near Cape Canaveral; midway down the page he notes:

"No rivers of any note fall into its northern branches, except St. Sebastians, directly opposite to whose mouth happened the shipwreck of the Spanish Admiral [sic], who was the northernmost wreck of fourteen galleons [sic], and a hired Dutch ship, all laden with specie and plate; which by stress of northeast winds were drove ashore and lost on this coast, between this place and the bleach-yard, in 1715. A hired Frenchman fortunately escaped by having steered half a point more east than the others. The people employed in the course of our survey, while walking the strand, after strong eastern gales, have repeatedly found pistareens and double pistareens, which kinds of money probably yet remaining in the wrecks, are sometimes washed up by the surf in hard winds. This Lagoon stretches parallel to the sea, until the latitude 27:20, where it has an out-watering, or mouth: directly before this mouth, in three-fathom water, lie the remains of the Dutch wreck. The banks of this lagoon are not fruitful."

Romans spelled it out, but it would be a long time before anyone paid attention to this particular piece of information. Centuries passed; storms, wars and generations came and went, but the sand and the sea kept their secret well. Occasionally, however, the elements revealed more clues — a few encrusted silver coins dredged up from the bottom and tossed on the beach or eroded from the dunes by a storm tide, a scattering of pottery fragments washed from the soil by a heavy rain, a shell-encrusted iron cannon uncovered by a rampaging surf. The clues were there for anyone capable of interpreting them. And eventually someone proved capable.

The forebears of our modem treasure hunters were simply people with a penchant for picking up the odd items the sea sometimes casts ashore. These weekend beachcombers were not treasure hunters in the usual sense: they were curio hunters. But the germ was there. All it needed was a little encouragement. Once someone had identified a blackened, misshapen wafer of metal as a Spanish piece of eight, the die was cast. Once local inhabitants had noted the frequency with which strange coins appeared along a lonely stretch of beach, it was not difficult to let one's imagination run to Spanish galleons and shipwrecked treasure fleets lost somewhere "out there." The legends and rumors persisted, and so did the growing number of weekend beachcombers. They came, they searched and they left again, rarely any richer for the experience and seldom any wiser. Yet among them were a few notable exceptions, men who followed the clues several steps further and found answers to the centuries-old mystery.

One of the first was amateur historian Charles D. Higgs, a retired astronomer who had spent many years surveying the Florida area for early historical materials. In 1941, his researches led him to the Cape Canaveral region and eventually to a specific area on the offshore bar or island lying between the Indian River and the Atlantic Ocean from two to three miles south of Sebastian Inlet on Florida's east coast. There, curio hunters had been finding various articles belonging to the Spanish colonial period, and Higgs had come to investigate. He listened to the local legends, he studied the clues, he sifted the sands; when he had finished, he wrote of his findings in a report he read to the archaeology session of the annual meeting of the Florida Historical Society on March 6, 1942.

"Down in the Indian River country, several miles below Cape Canaveral," reported Higgs, "there lies, half buried in the shifting sands, a sizable portion of a wrecked ship. This for some years has been ballyhooed as that of a Spanish galleon although its construction would render such belief very dubious. [Higgs based his belief on his observation that the seasonal growth rings evident in both the ribs and the planking of the wreck suggest our own northern woods rather than those of continuous growth that would have been used in the Spanish and Spanish-Indies ship construction. An eminent tropical forestry expert in Miami who examined specimens from the wreck expressed a similar opinion. Yet, noted Higgs, local legend had even associated this wreck with a fleet of the Adelantado (First Spanish governor of Florida) himself, with all the usual connotations of treasure.] It is my firm conviction that this particular hulk has no connection whatsoever with the findings in this report. It may, however, be quite pertinent to these findings that in placid weather other wrecks may be discerned along the adjacent reefs and shallows. Several cannon have been retrieved along the beach, and under favorable conditions of weather and tides, beachcombers and treasure hunters have picked up various articles of naval equipment and other relics undoubtedly of the Spanish colonial period." [Charles D. Higgs, "Spanish Contacts with the Ais (Indian River) Country," Florida Historical Quarterly, 21 (1942), 25-39. The founder of St. Augustine and first Spanish governor of Florida, Pedro Menendez de Aviles.]

During his investigation Higgs had been told that brass culverins (a kind of heavy cannon used in the 16th and 17th centuries), which from the description might be Spanish, had been removed. All the cannon he had personally seen were of a later period, though he noted certain characteristics that indicated they were made before 1800.

His curiosity aroused by this knowledge, Higgs took a closer look at the bluff behind the beach, searching for some clue. As he moved along the sandy escarpment paralleling the coast, he suddenly found what he was searching for. Four-tenths of a mile south of the wreck, a portion of the bluff had been eroded away by the wind and rain. Protruding from the sand were pieces of human and animal bones. The bluff at this point was from twelve to fourteen feet high. A little poking around revealed iron spikes, clay pipes and a peculiar assortment of pottery sherds. A scrutiny of this escarpment showed an abundance of this material, stretching back toward Indian River and along the bluff for some 500 feet. Later Higgs found that the fragments were scattered through the sand all the way to the river, a distance of some 800 feet from the Atlantic side of the bluff. Their relation to the rate of erosion and sea encroachment clearly indicated to Higgs that the site was formerly centered more conspicuously on the river than on the ocean front.

Searching for more clues, Higgs dug a few test holes a short distance back from the bluff and found the ground increasingly fertile in European artifacts. The material lay in a stratum of charcoal-impregnated beach sand two and a half to three feet thick. He established a point of reference at the approximate center of the site, then worked outward from it. Attempting to plot his finds on a grid, he found the procedure "rather purposeless, as there is every evidence that the site had been destroyed and scattered by storms prior to its burial in the drifting sands."

Hoping that a competent archaeological survey might later be made of the area, Higgs disturbed the site as little as possible, limiting his work to sifting the piles of loose debris left by treasure and souvenir hunters. Yet he obviously wondered just how worthwhile further study would be when he wrote: "Since the finding of relics here has become common knowledge, perhaps much of the station's archaeological value has been and is being destroyed, and inevitably, key findings dispersed."

Higgs had unknowingly found what was left of the southern portion of the old Spanish salvage and survivors' camp. It had been damaged by storms, partially eroded, and mauled by curio hunters; yet in the rubble that remained there were still tantalizing clues.

As the evidence mounted, Higgs discarded the idea that his finds were debris from a shipwreck, because the site was on a bluff ten to twelve feet above sea level. He thought instead that he had found some evidence of a European structure having been built there. "At the center of the station," he said, "there is a considerable area of tabby floor at a depth of three and one half feet. [What Higgs thought were the remains of a crushed shell floor were large lenses of compacted oyster shells from intensive Ays Indian occupation years before the loss of the 1715 fleet.] Beneath this floor is found an occasional sherd of incised or stamped Indian pottery. The choicest of the Spanish remains lie above and scattered around at a higher level; while still higher, about a foot below the surface, there is an abundance of the cruder, undecorated, recent Indian pottery. Scattered over a distance of 320 feet along the bluff there are four other deposits rich in brick and mortar fragments. It is only in the vicinity of the floor in the center of the station that the largest assortment of European articles is found, particularly the finer Spanish pottery and Chinese porcelain fragments."

The appearance of several varieties of Chinese porcelain at the site puzzled Higgs. In attempting to explain its presence, he made a surprisingly accurate observation: "We might suggest that the period involved was concurrent with the china mania in Europe…china was of great value, and doubtless many treasure ships from the Philippines carried it in cargo. This was packed overland from Acapulco and transshipped at Vera Cruz into homebound fleets, vessels from which might later be wrecked in the Bahamas Channel."

Higgs also found quantities of various old glass fragments, mostly bottlenecks with lead screw-tops and the bottoms of "spirit" bottles; Indian pottery; Spanish crockery from grain, oil and water jars; Spanish pottery — mostly glazed in blues, greens and browns; Spanish-Mexican pottery glazed inside and out; clay pipes bearing the trademark "R. Tippet" in cartouche, or the lettering "R.T." or "R.R." — the former was later found to be an 18th-century English pipe maker. Heavily corroded iron objects were the most common items he uncovered, but with the exception of ships' spikes, they were rusted beyond recognition. The cannon he identified at the site was later turned over to officials at St. Augustine.

Higgs's work was intentionally preliminary. He drew no conclusions from his finds. He knew, however, that the area had once been the territory of the Ays Indians, and his earlier research indicated that the tribe often enriched itself on gold and silver taken from Spanish treasure ships lost along their coast. The shipwreck evidence Higgs examined in the dunes was apparently too recent to be scientifically significant, nor did he venture a guess at why there might have been an early European structure built in this hostile land.

The amateur historian knew more than he was telling, however, or at least more than appeared in his published report. A study of Higgs's work papers for the 1940-1942 period indicates that he had seen a copy of Bernard Romans's 1775 chart of east Florida on which the English cartographer had printed this notation near the St. Sebastian River: "Opposite this River, perished the Admiral, commanding the Plate Fleet of 1715, the rest of the fleet, 14 in number, between this & Ye Bleech Yard." Nearby were the words "el Palmar," followed by tiny drawings of five palm trees. On a portion of a U.S. Coast and Geodetic Survey chart for this area, Higgs marked the exact location of the wreck near Sebastian Inlet, which years later would be known as the "Cabin Wreck." He also pinpointed the locations of several other wrecks of the 1715 fleet further south. The historian's work papers indicate that he had found examples of "clipped Mexican silver real coins" on the land site he was investigating, but again this fact did not appear in the historical-quarterly report. The oversight may have been intentional in that Higgs was not interested in encouraging treasure hunters to despoil the site further. Whatever answers there were to the riddle, however, he knew would have to come from a more detailed archaeological search of the area.

Four years elapsed before this occurred. Then, in 1946, Dr. Hale G. Smith, acting as Assistant Archaeologist for the Florida Park Service, took an archaeological team to the Higgs site. Accompanied by Higgs, Smith surveyed the area. The island was so densely covered with palmetto, sea grape, yucca and cabbage-palm growth that the team was forced to confine its efforts mainly to the beach escarpment, where it was clear enough to work. Their test trenches revealed that the site ran not less than 343 feet along the escarpment and 800 feet across the width of the island on the east-west excavation axis established by Higgs in 1942. Carefully digging and sifting five-foot squares along these base lines, the workers found their greatest concentration of artifacts nine to twenty-one inches below the surface. Most of the Indian pottery sherds were a type called San Marcos, which has been assigned by archaeologists to the St. Augustine Period (1565-1750). A partially formed stone pipe made from limestone, similar to fragments found around the site, was uncovered 213 feet south of the east-west axis. Eventually, the archaeologists' painstaking efforts turned up animal bones shaped into crude tools; a variety of Mexican ceramics; clay figurines; Chinese porcelain; Spanish and what were then referred to as "Moorish" ceramics, but which are now called Majolica or tin-glazed wares; glass from old wine and case-gin bottles; a handmade stemmed goblet; clay pipes; three bone or ivory dice; nails; spikes; knife blades; iron bands from chests; "line snubbers" for mooring boats; buckles; parts of flintlock pistols and lead musket balls. In addition there were limestone building materials, an alabaster bottle stopper and two coins bearing the Spanish coat of arms with the quartered lions and castles of Leon and Castile.

Smith now had a few more clues. The big question in his mind was how these objects came to be there. Remember, neither Higgs nor Smith knew the history of what had taken place on the Barra de Ays. They had only a few pieces of a complicated puzzle from which they dared to reconstruct the past. It would be many years before the full story of those historic events would be revealed from long forgotten documents buried in Spanish archives. Yet the archaeologist's deductions were remarkably accurate.

To explain his mixed collection of European and Indian artifacts. Smith saw three possibilities: 1) The Higgs site was once an aboriginal Indian village which continued to exist after the arrival of the Europeans; 2) it was a European settlement which drew the Indians to it; or, 3) the Europeans and a group of Indians, not necessarily native to the region, settled there simultaneously. Since the Indian, Spanish, Mexican and Chinese artifacts were all found in the same occupational stratum, he reasoned that the Europeans and Indians had lived there at the same time—and wondered when and why.

Smith's training as an anthropologist specializing in archaeology uniquely qualified him to date the artifacts. Still, he needed assistance with the rare porcelains. Corresponding with Kamer Agla Oglu, an expert on Chinese porcelain, he learned that the majority of these fragments from the site were of the K'ang Hsi period and made between 1662 and 1722. This indicated that the site could not have been established earlier than 1662. The Spanish-Mexican ware dated from the period 1543-1723, indicating that the site had probably not been occupied much later than 1723. An English clay pipe marked "R. Tippet" was made in the early 18th century. Considering only these three items. Smith narrowed the date of the site to a fifty-year period between 1675 and 1725. When he learned from his research that the English Quaker Jonathan Dickinson had not reported any European settlement in that area when he passed through in 1696, he reduced the probable range even more, to 1697-1725. Still, the presence of the English pipes bothered him. What were they doing in a predominantly Spanish site? The Spanish had never been a pipe-smoking group, and few of their red clay pipes had been found in Florida. Also, considering the friction between the two countries, he thought it doubtful that the Spanish were getting pipes from the English. [Smith was working in the formative period of Florida archaeology. It would be many years before our knowledge of Spanish shipwrecks and salvage camps would enable archaeologists to expect that up to 20 percent or more of the artifacts from such "Spanish sites" would, during this period, tend to be of English origin.]

These facts suggested to Smith the possibility that the site may have been an intermittent hangout for pirates—probably English or Dutch. It was known that the English and Dutch privateers traded with the Ays and used their inlets as bases for their raids against Spanish shipping. Besides affording good harbors, these places offered a source of fresh water that was out of reach of the nearest Spanish garrison.

The next very significant piece of evidence was Bernard Romans's reference to the loss of the 1715 Spanish Plate Fleet on his 1775 Florida chart, accompanied by the words "el Palmar." From an old Spanish source given him by Higgs, Smith learned that in 1716, a year after the Plate Fleet wreck, there was supposedly a pirates' hangout at "Palmar de Ays." Surely this was the same "el Palmar" shown on Romans's chart.

Summing up the results of his research in 1949, Smith wrote:

> Earlier, using the Dickinson data and the dating from the artifacts, we came to the conclusion that the site must fall between 1696 and 1725. Here we have two documentary references [Romans's chart and the Spanish mention of pirates at the Palmar de Ays] which would readily explain the amount of European material present in the area, and dating from about the middle of the postulated time range. Considering all the data it seems very likely that the Higgs site represents materials from the Plate Fleet of 1715 and/or the pirates' hangout of the following year. It must also be borne in mind that Indians, possibly Ays [and in a footnote he included Yamasee] were associated with the site, probably drawn there by the wrecks. [Hale G. Smith, "Two Archaeological Sites in Brevard County, Florida," Florida Anthropological Society Publications, No. 1 (Gainesville: University of Florida, 1949).]

Smith could not have been closer to the truth.

Chapter 9

The Trail to Treasure-Trove

The next character to figure in this drama was a building contractor from Miamisburg, Ohio, named Kip Wagner.

At the end of World War II, Wagner came to the small east-coast Florida town of Wabasso to build a motel. Wabasso is six miles from Sebastian, and both communities are situated in the general area shown on the Romans chart as the Palmar de Ays. Wagner said that when he arrived in the area, he had no clearer idea about treasure hunting than anyone else whose only association with the subject was a vaguely remembered youthful enthusiasm for Robert Louis Stevenson's Treasure Island. But if anything could rekindle that enthusiasm, it was the stories of treasure lost and treasure found that Wagner heard from old-timers in the Wabasso-Sebastian area. What particularly interested him was the rumors that blackened Spanish coins sometimes turned up on the beach after a howling northeast gale.

Captain Steadman A. Parker was apparently the first to tell Wagner about the coins. Parker, a retired steamship captain, was renowned in the area for his thrilling tales about transatlantic crossings and European adventures. He told Wagner that a Spanish treasure fleet had foundered on the coast nearby, and over the years the long-lost treasure kept washing ashore just east of Wabasso. Parker said he had found some of the coins on the beach. Furthermore, the ex-sea captain insisted that there was a big treasure somewhere offshore just waiting to be found and that one day he intended to find it.

Wagner said he did not know whether to believe the story or not, but one weekend he surreptitiously spent an afternoon at the beach looking for coins and finding nothing but seashells. The experience did not allay his curiosity, however, especially after his hearing other yarns from scattered sources. Whether fact or fiction, they fired Wagner's imagination and whetted his curiosity even more. There was, for example, the postmaster of Sebastian who in the early 1900s was said to have found a fortune in silver and gold coins, which he kept hidden in a cigar box until the night he was murdered. The box and hoarded coins were never found. Another tale concerned a Mr. Kragle who ferried mail from the mainland to an island in the Indian River near Sebastian Inlet and once saw cannon on the bottom during one of his trips. It was also reported that he once found a heavy "brick" in shallow water and used it in building a fireplace. The first time he started a fire, the brick melted. And then there was the old man who Wagner said told him he had found plenty of the blackened odd-shaped pieces of metal on the beach. He didn't know what they were, but he said their shape made them fine "skipping stones" when he sailed them out to sea — as he judged he had done with some two thousand of them.

In 1949 the ex-steamer captain, Steadman Parker, told Wagner that he had located the remains of a shipwreck near shore. Wagner and three others quit their jobs and agreed to help him recover it. First they used a dragline on shore and tried to scoop up the wreck from the shallow water. When this failed, they bulldozed piles of sand into the Atlantic, and at low tide moved the dragline out on to this makeshift pier in an effort to extend its reach. Each full tide washed away their sandy platform, and each day they rebuilt it. It was during one of these times that the bulldozer unearthed a coin, but according to Wagner it was a Spanish copper maravedi dated 1649, which he said he later gave away to one of the workers more impressed with it than he.

By summer's end, the group's salvage attempt had proved to be an expensive fiasco. After dredging up tons of ocean bottom, the men had found only a few wood fragments, ships' fastenings and metal spikes. They gave up and returned to their jobs.

But the following spring Wagner again felt the urge to search. Borrowing an old Army-surplus metal detector from Parker, he prowled the ocean front between Wabasso and Sebastian Inlet. As the summer passed, the detector zeroed him in on the usual junk — rusty tin cans, bottle caps and other useless items. Then, one day, the instrument enabled him to discover his first silver coin. It was an 8 real the size of a half dollar. At that moment, Kip Wagner became addicted to treasure hunting.

In the following months he found other coins, but his method was slow and plodding. His hunting ground was the six-mile strip of sand between Wabasso and Sebastian Inlet. It was a desolate coast where the full tide always lapped the dunes, while the ebb tide left a smoothly washed strand just a hundred feet wide. On weekends Wagner avoided the beach, then dotted with vacationers. But during the week, when the visitors were gone, he usually had the place to himself. Then he worked at his leisure, trudging the long, empty miles under a hot, glaring sun while he studied the beach. Nothing escaped his eyes. He learned to skim debris, broken shells and rusty bottle caps at a glance, hardly seeing them. But if among those items he glimpsed even the partially exposed edge of an irregular black shape, he subconsciously glanced back at it, singling it out for closer investigation. At least forty times in the next few months, these objects were old Spanish coins. Before long he had a small collection of the heavy, sulphided pieces of eight and a few small irregular gold coins. These he hoarded like a miser, lest word get out and Federal agents make him turn in the precious metal to the government. Years later Wagner learned that hidden or unclaimed objects found on the beach are considered treasure- trove and not liable to seizure. Meanwhile, however, he jealously guarded his growing collection and continued to beachcomb the productive strip of sand between Wabasso and Sebastian Inlet, which he fondly called his "money beach."

As his finds increased, so did Wagner's curiosity about where they had come from. Had the coins always lain on the beach, or were the waves of a storm-driven Atlantic casting them up from somewhere offshore? Wagner waded around in the surf, dragging his feet and trying to find other coins, but with no success. Still, he felt that they were washing in.

One of his close associates in those days, Dr. Kip Kelso, disagreed, believing the old coins had lain for centuries under the sand of the beach until the pounding surf unearthed them. Wagner apparently resolved the question by hiring a ditch-digging machine and digging three separate trenches seventy-five feet long and several feet deep across a usually productive stretch of beach. When no coins appeared, he and Kelso were convinced that the pieces of eight were washing ashore. After that, the two men got down to some serious treasure hunting.

First they had to establish what exactly they were looking for—a broken chest of coins, a single wreck or an entire fleet? When and where was the treasure-trove lost?

The best clues they had were the coins themselves. None that Wagner had found or had seen in other people's collections was dated later than 1715. As the two men cast about for information, someone told Wagner that a Spanish fleet carrying $14,000,000 in treasure had gone down in a hurricane off Cape Canaveral in 1715. But when he sent a 1714 coin to the Smithsonian Institution and asked if it was possible that the silver piece could have come from that fleet, the response was confusing. Mendel Peterson replied that the coin could not have come from that fleet, since it had been sunk 150 miles farther south in the Florida Keys, a sinking about which he was then writing a book. Treasure maps circulating during this time commonly carried a notation indicating that the fleet lost in 1715 had sunk on Carysfort Reef off Key Largo.

After receiving that news, Wagner and Kelso decided they had better start doing some research of their own. Instead of searching the beach, they started searching their local libraries, reading everything they could find that had anything to do with treasure or shipwrecks off the Florida east coast. Not surprisingly, they found themselves mired in records covering many such wrecks, but not one fitted the picture of a fleet sinking in a hurricane near Sebastian Inlet in 1715.

Finally, after a fruitless search of several Florida libraries, Kelso went to Washington to see what he could find in the Library of Congress. One of the works he encountered there was A Survey of Indian River Archaeology by Professor Irving Rouse of Yale. In it Rouse not only gives a detailed account of the 1715 fleet disaster on the Barra de Ays but also discusses the work of Higgs and Smith. The author mentions as one of his sources Bernard Romans's A Concise Natural History of East and West Florida, published in 1775. Kelso quickly located the volume in the library's rare-book collection and so was in possession of the information that many people, it appears, had had but no one had yet put to use.

Romans's book and chart established the general area of the shipwrecks. Now Wagner and Kelso needed more specific information. What were the circumstances surrounding the disaster? What and how much treasure had the various ships carried? Had any of it already been salvaged?

From reading various treasure-hunting books, Wagner learned that the richest storehouse of Spanish-American historical documents is the General Archives of the Indies in Seville, Spain. He wrote its curator, Dr. Jose de la Pena, requesting specific information about the 1715 fleet. When the reply arrived, the treasure hunters were disappointed to find that it told them nothing about the fleet that they did not already know.

They tried again, this time through a friend who was visiting Spain and who agreed to talk to Dr. Pena and show him some of the silver coins they had found.

Months passed before they learned that this direct approach had been successful. The welcome result, according to Wagner, was 30 feet of microfilmed documents written in archaic Spanish that detailed the background of the late-17th- and early-18th-century Spanish treasure fleets. With the occasional help of National Park Service historian Luis R. Arana, an authority on archaic Spanish, Wagner and Kelso took about a year to decipher most of the script and translate it into English. But the effort bore fruit. The documents provided the names and numbers of the ships, their sailing dates and routes, and the events surrounding the loss of the fleet in 1715. What particularly pleased the treasure hunters was the remarkably detailed manifest lists recording the silver, gold and jewelry the fleet had carried; 14 million pesos worth of treasure.

Fragmentary though it was, the story was there, including references to the early salvage camp and the amount of treasure the Spanish had successfully salvaged.

With these clues and a war-surplus metal detector, Wagner intensified his search of the beaches, hoping to pinpoint the old Spanish salvage camp. If he could find that, he supposed he would be within reach of the wrecks. His excursions into the thick palmetto and cabbage-palm undergrowth on the bluffs behind the beach brought him eventually to a sandy depression that looked more man-made than natural. He started working over the area with his metal detector and within an hour had turned up a ship's spike and a cannonball. Then he began marking the places that gave his detector the highest readings. The metal concentrations were spotted over half an acre.

What Wagner had stumbled onto was the Higgs site, which the amateur historian had investigated in 1940-1942 and Hale Smith had worked archaeologically in 1946, concentrating his efforts mainly along the beach escarpment because of the area's dense undergrowth.

Apparently unaware of the University of Florida's historical and anthropological publications concerning the site, Wagner wrote the South Florida Historical Society, explaining what he had found and asking for an opinion. The Society sent two of its representatives, who looked over the area, examined his finds and agreed that the place could be the old Spanish campsite.

With that green light, Wagner went to work. He posted off a half acre of the land, hired a bulldozer to clear away the palmettos, then settled down to shoveling and sifting his way through the sand. By the end of several months' hard work he had uncovered hundreds of fragments of Mexican ceramics, Chinese porcelain, Spanish olive jars, bricks and some cannonballs. His finds were almost identical with those of Higgs and Smith, with these notable exceptions: Wagner also unearthed parts of a small early-19th-century coffee mill, a bullet mold, musket balls, a pair of rusty cutlasses lying inches apart as if they had been in a leather case, three rectangular fragments of blackened silver, thirteen silver pieces of eight and a crudely made gold ring with a 2 1/2-carat diamond mounted in it and six tiny diamonds set around the band. This last was his most valuable find.

Diver brandishes an encrusted sword.

Cannons are hoisted by their dolphins.

Two sets of 8, 4, 2, and 1 real 18th Century silver coins.

Clump of corroded silver coins in the shape of their bag.

Scattering of gold doubloons.

A morning's find of gold coins placed on a diver's wetsuit top.

Finders Keepers Losers Weepers.

Wagner with silver wedges that fit into a barrel.

Salvor Tom Gurr's work boat.

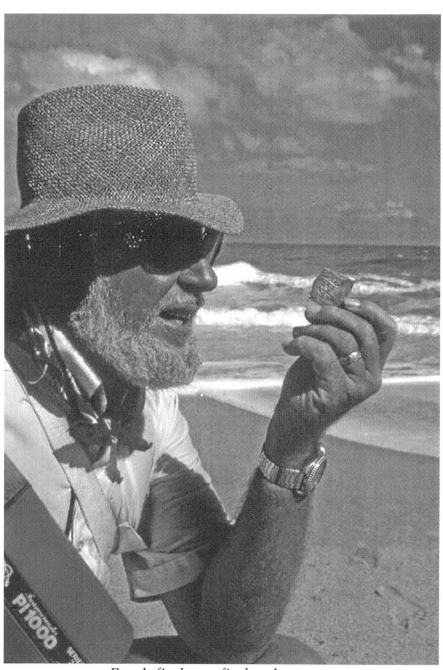

Beach finds are finders keepers.

Occasionally, Wagner broke the routine of his work ashore to swim out through the surf and look at the bottom through a window he had installed in a homemade surfboard. He always went hoping to find a shipwreck, but he did not really have any idea what one would look like. One day, however, as he was paddling along looking at the bottom, he saw something he had not seen before. Just below him, in eight feet of water, was a cannon. Beside it were four more. Wagner quickly dove down to inspect them. Each cannon was about nine feet long. Though they were covered with a brown patina of marine growth, there was no mistaking what they were. Nearby lay a huge ship's anchor. Wagner stayed with his find until his breath gave out; then he surfaced, panting more from excitement than exertion. To be certain not to lose the spot, he lined it up with marks on shore. Then he swam ashore and bulldozed through the palmettos a swath that pointed straight at the spot.

Now that he had found what he suspected might be a wreck site, he wondered if there might be others nearby. Thinking that perhaps he could spot them more quickly from the air, he leased a single-engine Taylor-Craft and had the pilot fly him along the beach while he squinted at the shallows below. Whenever he sighted unidentifiable objects or peculiar dark areas on the bottom, he dropped weighted coconuts to mark them. Then he had the plane land on the beach so that he could swim out and examine the areas more closely. Both Higgs and Smith had written that wrecks could be seen in the calm waters adjacent to the campsite, and Wagner found this to be true. But the coast was so littered with shipwreck debris that he could not tell the difference between the old and the new.

Wagner acquired swim fins, mask and scuba gear and made several dives on the wreck site south of Sebastian Inlet. As he looked over the bottom he realized that if there was any real treasure to be found there, salvaging it was going to be a bigger job than he could handle alone. The wreckage was badly scattered, most of it buried under the sand. It would take men, money and machinery for a proper salvage job, and these things were then beyond his reach. The best he could do for the time being was make a mental note of the wreck's size and distribution. The rest would have to wait until another day.

Wagner himself, however, did not wait. He went to Fort Pierce to investigate another site. This was a shipwreck so well known that almost every skin diver in the area had dived to it. Wagner swam out to it several times to see what he could find. The site contained tons of ballast rocks, a formidable barrier to anyone curious about what might he beneath them. Wagner reported that his repeated trips netted him a handful of 1715 silver coins, but again he knew that any serious salvage effort would require assistance. He said he then made up his mind that he either had to find what he needed or get out of the treasure-hunting "business" entirely. And at that point Wagner was not about to quit. He believed he was sitting on the biggest jackpot of his life; all he lacked was the means to secure it.

But there were other considerations. So far his treasure-hunting activities had been on a relatively small scale. He knew that when he went into it in a big way, he would have to observe certain legalities; for example, securing the right to salvage on state-owned submerged land. In preparation for that day, he decided to make application to the state for a search-salvage lease.

In Tallahassee Wagner met Van H. Ferguson, director of Florida's Internal Improvement Fund and discussed his plans with him. He said he was interested in working several sites on the Florida east coast and would like to make application for the necessary lease. Ferguson outlined the prerequisites for such an agreement and discussed its various parts with Wagner to be sure he understood what was involved. Simply stated, the standard policy then in effect was that the governor of the state of Florida, and his cabinet, as owners of all submerged lands under the state's navigable waters, could lease the same for search or salvage operations. A single lease could not include more than fifty square miles of submerged land, but other leases of land within the area could be secured until a specific find was made; then the lessee might define a one-acre area and request that his lease of this area be exclusive so that no other individual could work it. The cost of the annual lease was $100, payable in advance. In addition, the agreement called for a $500 bond and quarterly reports to the Florida Internal Improvement Fund detailing operations and listing all finds. For granting this search and salvage privilege, the state would retain 25 percent of whatever was recovered from the submerged land (subject to state selection). If the lessee broke any of the terms of the agreement by either failing to report finds truthfully or selling or otherwise disposing of finds before making a division with the state, then the lease would be subject to forfeiture and cancellation by the state.

The arrangement satisfying Wagner, Ferguson started the paperwork in 1959. Wagner's application to the Florida Internal Improvement Fund was for an exploration lease covering a fifty-mile area from Sebastian Inlet to a point near Stuart, Florida, with exclusive pinpoint salvage-right leases on the specific wreck sites he had investigated. As Wagner recalled later, applying for the lease was one of the smartest moves he ever made.

Chapter 10

Cannon's Silver Pie

In 1959 a series of events occurred that would have a long-lasting effect on the future of Florida treasure hunting. The catalyst responsible for this chain reaction was Boston-born Louis J. Ullian, who grew up in Fort Lauderdale, Florida. Like most boys, Ullian was steeped in stories of pirates and treasure-trove, but unlike most he lived within sight of the old Spanish Plate Fleets' homebound treasure route and was accustomed to beachcombing for pieces of eight along the ocean front by the time he was twelve years old.

With a degree in mechanical engineering from Purdue University, he joined the Navy in 1955. Knowledge he gained in handling explosives during some of his diving experiences brought him an assignment to ordnance engineering, and he was trained in the disposal of explosive ordnance. When he completed his service in 1959, this training qualified him for the job of Ordnance Engineer at the Air Force Missile Test Range at Cape Canaveral. Each time the Air Force fired a rocket there, Ullian was responsible for seeing that its destruct system was operative in the event that range officers deemed it necessary to destroy the rocket before it threatened land areas.

Whenever time and finances permitted, however, Ullian continued his hobby of treasure hunting. He had explored what he believed to be the wreck of a 1733 Spanish treasure ship and over the years had found just enough artifacts and adventure to whet his appetite for more.

One day in 1959, Ullian stepped into the diving shop at the base and met the owner, Delphine Long, a diving enthusiast with a talent for repairing anything mechanical. Long was the ground power equipment supervisor at Patrick Air Force Base, but his real love was the sea. He had organized a skin-diving club at the base and in 1958 had actually poked around in the ballast rock and scattered debris of the 1715 wreck near Sebastian Inlet without knowing what he had found.

Since the two shared an interest in diving and bottom-scratching for artifacts. Long persuaded Ullian to join his diving club. Several days later at a meeting Ullian met Ervin Taylor, another diver, who lived at Micco, near Sebastian. When Ullian described some of his treasure-hunting experiences in southern Florida, Taylor mentioned that he lived near someone whom he thought Ullian should meet. He said the man's name was Kip Wagner and that he had been hunting treasure for years.

The four men eventually got together at Wagner's home and talked treasure. For many nights through the winter of 1959-1960, they met and compared notes, examined one another's finds and discussed the methods that might be used to salvage the sites Wagner was eager to explore. They planned to try a group effort the coming spring, pooling their manpower and equipment to see what they could do. But when they took stock of what each of them had to offer the enterprise, it became obvious that they lacked the essentials for even a modest operation. They needed help in both manpower and equipment.

Finding divers willing to go treasure hunting was no problem, but finding reliable persons who had something more than diving experience to offer the venture was another thing. But Lou Ullian had someone in mind—Colonel Dan F. Thompson, one of his bosses at the base. Thompson was not only an expert diver but a graduate electrical engineer

136

finishing up a distinguished twenty-four-year career in the Air Force as director of operations at the missile test center. When Ullian told him of their plans, Thompson was eager to join the group.

The next recruit was Lieutenant Colonel Harry Cannon, who worked for Thompson as chief of the Range Safety Office. Cannon's Air Force experiences included flying B-24s and C-47s over the Himalayas from India to China during World War II. After the war he was trained extensively in electronics and communications. In 1959, one of his jobs at the Cape was to push the destruct button on any wayward rocket and blow up the multimillion-dollar missile before it got into trouble. Cannon was also in charge of a special task force for recovering astronauts downed at sea, but he was not a diver. He owned a twenty-one-foot boat that the treasure hunters felt would be useful for ferrying them to the wreck sites. And shortly after joining the group he was initiated into the mysteries of diving. One cold night in January his companions strapped him into scuba gear, briefed him on what he was supposed to do, then tossed him into the icy waters of the Officers Club swimming pool. Cannon quickly became an accomplished diver.

There were now eight of them. They all came from different backgrounds and they were all skilled in an interesting assortment of specialties — Louis Ullian, diver, treasure hunter, explosives expert and ex-Navy ordnance engineer; Delphine Long, diver, treasure hunter, mechanical and electrical specialist; Ervin Taylor, diver and top mechanic; Colonel Dan Thompson, diver, electrical engineer, legal and organizational expert; Lieutenant Colonel Harry Cannon, diver, communications and electronics specialist with a flair for handling business and financial matters; Lisbon Futch, a skilled boatsman with wide knowledge of the channels and shoals in the Sebastian area; Dr. Kip Kelso, scholar and researcher well informed in Spanish history; and Kip Wagner, experienced in the one field in which they all shared a common interest—treasure hunting.

Considering the kind of operation he had in mind, Wagner wondered how well they would work together. Could they stand the long hours, the months of hard work, the probable obstacles and the possible dangers that lay ahead? Or when the going got tough, would they quit in disgust?

Wagner felt that he had to know. He had invested too much in the project to risk losing it because his group of eager treasure hunters could not stand the pressures. Instead of putting them on his choice site south of Sebastian Inlet, he decided to test them first on the picked-over Fort Pierce wreck, where he knew the work would be hard, the obstacles many and the chances of finding treasure virtually nil. If they could weather that, then they would be ready for the real thing.

On a cold, blustery day in January 1960, the group made its first of many exploratory runs out to the wreck north of Fort Pierce in Cannon's cabin cruiser to size up the situation. Enthusiasm compensated for what the fledgling treasure salvagers lacked in equipment. As they peered down through three fathoms of water at the huge pile of heavy ballast rock littering the site, the men were far more speculative about the rewards that might lie beneath that formidable mountain of rocks than about the prodigious job of moving it. Wagner suspected that whatever finds were there would be few and far between; yet he found his friends' excitement infectious. Scores of divers had visited the site, but he doubted that anyone had ever made a thorough search of it. Who could tell what might still be there?

In the weekends that followed, they made repeated trips to the wreck to scout it from above. Meanwhile they scrounged for diving equipment—tanks, regulators, fins, face masks, weight belts—gradually acquiring what they needed, repairing and pooling what they had.

Their greatest need was for a work boat large enough to

hold them, their diving equipment and some of the more sophisticated salvage gear they hoped to build. Libe Futch solved the problem when he went to the salvage yards at Norfolk, Virginia, and bought them a forty-foot Navy liberty launch. The boat was little more than a paint-chipped, soot-begrimed hull. But they scraped, patched, painted and overhauled it, added a deck and canopy, and dubbed it the Sampan. When they had finished, the vessel looked less like a fugitive from a junkyard and more like a work boat that would do the job for them.

The mechanically minded members of the group improvised a two-inch sand dredge built from junkyard parts. Powered by a tractor engine mounted on the bow of the boat, a pump shot a stream of water through a fire hose connected to the lower end of a piece of stovepipe, creating the suction necessary to vacuum sand from the bottom. It was a Rube Goldberg contraption, but it worked. With this and other pieces of patched or makeshift equipment, the group launched itself into the treasure-salvage business. That March, Wagner received the salvage lease he had applied for almost a year earlier. Every weekend after that was spent on the Fort Pierce wreck, and there was nothing glamorous about what the men did there. It was hard work. The pile of ballast rock that had been carried in the ship's hull to stabilize the vessel was seventy feet long, twenty feet wide and eight feet deep. By midsummer they had cut a ten-foot swath through the middle of it, removing the rock stone by stone, averaging four to five hundred a day. When they reached bottom, the nozzle of the homemade sand dredge was sent down to start eating into the sand. The divers hovered over it anxiously, hoping to see something of value appear. But as the pale yellow grains of sand were sucked up the pipe and discharged a short distance away, there was nothing. The hole grew deeper and the divers grew more intent, but there was no fortune to be found that day. Nor was it to be found in the many days and the many new holes that followed. In the process they unearthed hundreds of pieces of broken Mexican pottery, tiny chips of blue and white china which were later identified as K'ang Hsi porcelain, a truckload of cannonballs, a copper rim and handle, timber fragments and a handful of brass nails. But no treasure.

With their initial enthusiasm slightly dampened, they moved their operations to another part of the ballast pile and started over again, bisecting the big rock heap with another hand-picked trench. As the summer slipped away they continued to burrow through the pile at a snail's speed, until by August they had crisscrossed it so many times with trenches that the ballast heap resembled a cut pie. They had increased their finds by several hundred more pieces of broken pottery and cannonballs, but still no treasure, not even so much as a single coin. By now everyone's spirits were so low that the only thing that kept them going was sheer stubbornness. Then, Harry Cannon found something that suddenly made it all worthwhile.

Cannon had been excavating a small hole of his own. When the endless chore of rock moving got too monotonous for him, he occasionally slipped away to poke around in his private sand pit. Later, when the others asked him why he persisted in working that one place. Cannon's only comment was that it looked interesting to him.

One day toward the end of the diving season. Cannon left the rock-moving detail and swam off by himself to probe his private place. He had hardly started digging when his crowbar struck something hard. Reaching into the hole, he extracted a fist-sized wedge of blackened metal. Where his bar had scraped it he saw the gleam of silver. Cannon's first impulse was to rush to the surface with his find, but on second thought he returned to the hole, his heart beating in double time as he clawed at the sand. His efforts were rewarded with five more wedges. Then he tucked the pieces under his arms and swam up.

When the Sampan's crew saw his find they whooped for

joy. Cannon's wedges formed perfect silver "pie" eight inches in diameter. Someone estimated that a keg of wedges would probably be three layers deep and weigh around a hundred pounds. With that, everyone went over the side hellbent to find the missing layers. By day's end they had found three more wedges, making a total of eight—each one believed to be worth from $500 to $600.

The treasure find did wonders for the men. Their enthusiasm shot back up to normal. They were a close-knit team again, and Wagner decided that their test on the Fort Pierce wreck had amply proved their staying power. Now he felt they deserved to move on to bigger things; the Sebastian Inlet site. But that would have to wait until the following spring. Their diving season was over.

Chapter 11

Whence Came the Golden Dragon?

Those last cold months in 1960 were the longest they ever remembered. The divers itched to get into the water to see for themselves the secret site Wagner had saved for them. But it was out of the question. The wild surf was still on one of its prolonged winter rampages. All the men could do was stand on the beach and stare gloomily at the big waves smashing themselves to smithereens on the hidden limestone ledges flanking the area a few hundred yards offshore.

To keep their minds off the frustrating situation, Wagner kept them busy patching the boat and repairing their equipment. Then, on January 8, 1961, the seas momentarily calmed, and there was no holding the divers. Despite a fifteen-knot wind and frothing whitecaps, everyone piled into the Sampan and chugged out through the treacherous crosscurrents of narrow Sebastian Inlet to reconnoiter the site.

Beyond the pass the ocean was calmer, but the bone-chilling wind was whipping foaming combers over the first and second bars. The wreck site lay between them in the trough.

About 9 A.M. they reached the area two and a half miles south of the inlet and dropped anchor in the relatively calm water separating the two jagged upcropings of Anastasia limestone lying on either side of them. If the Sampan swung fifty to a hundred feet in either direction, it took no vivid imagination to visualize their being disemboweled on the same rocks that had sunk the ship they were seeking.

Cannon and Thompson, the only ones with wetsuits, went over the side to look at the bottom. Visibility below was less than an arm's length, and a strong swell was running. Each time it swept in, the divers grabbed for rock outcroppings to keep from being sucked along with it. If they happened to be caught in the open, the icy water sent them somersaulting toward shore. But in the brief calm between waves, they swam a serpentine pattern over the bottom, searching every shadow for signs of wreckage.

In minutes Cannon spotted something angular, dimly outlined below him. He swooped down to investigate. It was one of the three cannon Wagner had sighted earlier from his homemade surfboard. Cannon surfaced and signaled the Sampan to move closer. Then he hailed Thompson and jackknifed down for a closer inspection of the bottom.

Thompson never reached him. Halfway there, as he was fining along just over the rippled white sand, he began seeing scattered objects sticking up out of the bottom. The constant scouring of the big waves had apparently skimmed off several feet of loose overburden from the wreck site. Between trying to keep from being tumbled by the swell and avoiding being sucked out by the undertow, he spotted two curious rocklike objects about a foot and a half thick, and paused to examine them. The blackish green lumps were lightly encrusted with limestone, and he was unsure what they were. But he had no trouble identifying what lay around them in shallow sand pockets—single and clustered pieces of eight. Silver coins were scattered over the bottom, but he decided to salvage the two large objects, if only to learn what they were.

The problem was how to do it. Each of the lumps was almost too heavy to lift. If he swam up to call the boat, he might not find them again. But since that seemed the most logical solution, he surfaced and shouted for the Sampan.

144

Wagner and the others were having trouble hoisting the anchor. Thompson waited about ten minutes to see if they would get started, then dove back down to the bottom, where he almost panicked when he found he had drifted in the strong currents and could not immediately relocate the lumps. Minutes later he found them. He was determined not to leave them again.

Instead, he managed to get both of the bulky weights under his arms and started to walk the bottom toward the boat. After staggering some fifty feet, he was so winded he had to drop one of the lumps. He carried the other back to a rusty mast strap he had seen that might make a good marker. Then he quickly swam to retrieve the one he had dropped, intending to return it to the mast strap. That was when he made his second mistake. He could not find the lump he had dropped.

Thoroughly disgusted with himself, Thompson scooped up a handful of loose coins, swam for the Sampan, and flung the coins aboard with a muttered comment about their being so profuse on the bottom that he could collect them with a rake. Then he called for a line and dove again.

He had no trouble finding the mast strap and making the rope fast to the lump, but when he tried to lift the heavy weight while they hauled on the rope from above, the effort was almost too much for him. The lump swung dizzily in the currents, rising and dropping with the pitching boat.

Once on the surface, Thompson started the battle again, kicking furiously with his flippers to push the lump high enough for the others to drag it aboard. Finally, with everyone's help, the feat was accomplished. Thompson followed his find, completely exhausted.

It did not take them long to learn that he had found a cluster of corroded silver coins that weighed seventy-seven pounds and contained an estimated 1,500 to 2,000 pieces of eight.

They congratulated themselves hoarse.

As soon as Thompson caught his breath, he told them about the cluster he had lost. After that it made no difference how cold or rough the water was—divers tumbled off the boat in all directions. Seconds later they surfaced, clutching fistfuls of coins snatched from the bottom. Up and down they went, adding rapidly to the growing pile of silver accumulating on the Sampan. They stayed until their teeth chattered; they stayed until they turned blue. After forty-five icy minutes, one of the men found the lump Thompson had lost. Even then it took a blast of foul weather finally to drive them out of the water and force them back to port.

As they counted their day's take that evening, they found they had collected some four thousand silver pieces of eight.

Over the next few weeks, high seas and bad weather prevented the men from returning to the site. Then, when they did return, they were disappointed to find that everything on the bottom had changed. Visibility was about twelve inches, severe wave action had covered the wreck area with a layer of sand, and the coins were more difficult to find. But once the air lift was put to work, the divers were soon picking them up again.

Lou Ullian found a purplish-black lump, which he thought might be another cluster of coins. He examined it, chipping off a corner of the block with his crowbar. Since it looked like rock, he decided it was a piece of coral. He sat on it most of the morning, fanning the sand for coins.

That afternoon when Ullian and Thompson went down to take a last look around the bottom, Thompson spotted the large lump and pointed it out to Ullian, who simply shook his head.

Failing to understand him, Thompson turned the lump over and examined a side Ullian had apparently missed. There, in a small indentation, were the unmistakable shapes of coins.

Ullian's lump was a cluster of corroded coins later found to contain nearly two thousand silver pieces of eight estimated to be worth from $20,000 to $30,000.

Wagner and the others realized that the combined value of their recent finds removed them from the status of amateur treasure hunters. Now they qualified as pros. Since the business of harvesting coins had been so good, they decided to protect their interests by forming a corporation. They named it Real Eight, after the Spanish term for a piece of eight, ocho reales. The eight charter members elected officers, making Wagner president, and split a thousand shares of stock among them. After that, for better or worse, they were officially treasure hunters.

The next time they went to work, business could not have been worse. Even their cannon had disappeared. In January the cannon had been lying on the bottom in three fathoms of water. Now, a month later, only the surface buoys that had been tied to them remained, the lines running down to the bottom at two fathoms. That meant the cannon were buried under six feet of sand, thanks to the fickle currents, and so was the rest of the site. The divers would have to move tons of sand before they were in business again.

Once again the mechanical talents of Del Long and Erv Taylor were put to the test with the various sand-moving devices they had built from junk parts. Their first contraption was a two-inch sand pump that worked by centrifugal force. It ran well, but it ate sand too slowly. Their next invention was an air lift that used an old Model T Ford engine for a compressor. This malfunctioned so many times during the trial runs that it was discarded.

In May, Neptune apparently took pity on them, because the sea suddenly cleared the offending tons of sand from the site and left it as clean as before. Jubilantly the divers descended, gazed happily at their exposed cannon and spent the next four days familiarizing themselves with the distribution of the wreck. Before they could dig, however, Neptune changed his mind and once again covered the site with tons of sand.

That was the last straw. The group angrily resolved to find some kind of sand dredge that would do the job. Once again the mechanics cast about for ideas. Taylor had read about an injection dredge used by California divers searching for gold. It involved jetting a column of water up a pipe and creating a strong suction at the intake end for "sniffing" gold out of rock pockets and crevices. The idea looked practical, so Taylor fashioned a similar apparatus, a six-inch diameter, nine-foot-long aluminum tube. Instead of water, a jet of compressed air was shot up the inside of the tube by a two-and-a-half inch fire hose, and the resulting suction was powerful enough to burrow deep holes in the bottom within minutes. Any shells, coins or other treasure sucked up with the sand was caught in a screen basket attached to the outlet. On its trial run, with eighty to ninety pounds of air pressure powering it, the nine-foot-long tube whipped around the bottom like a berserk boa constrictor bent on tossing its operator off its business end. The monster gobbled everything within reach, including cannonballs and incautious hands. But once they learned how to control it, the divers found the dredge worked splendidly. So voracious was its appetite that they affectionately named their mechanical helper "The Hungry Beast."

During this period, Real Eight's relationship with the state was beyond reproach. To oversee the state's quarter share in all finds made, the Internal Improvement Fund selected two eminent archaeologists to work with the salvagers — Dr. William H. Sears, then curator of Social Sciences at the Florida State Museum in Gainesville, and Dr. John M. Goggin, head of the Anthropology Department at the University of Florida and the first professionally trained archaeologist to work in underwater archaeology.

The arrangement worked well. At the end of each diving season the salvagers met informally with the two archaeologists for a division of the treasure and artifacts. Goggin and Sears would select 25 percent of the find for the state's collection, and Wagner would load it into the back of his pickup truck and drive it to Gainesville for them. The articles selected by the two archaeologists consisted mainly of ships' fastenings and gear, armament such as cannon and musket balls, and ceramic fragments—artifacts of historical or scientific value from which archaeologists could reconstruct the past. The salvagers' share was coins and other items of greater material value. Both sides were satisfied with the arrangement. In a letter to the Internal Improvement Fund Director, Van Ferguson, on January 13, 1961, Sears stressed this point:

"The Real Eight Company is doing its work in a scientifically impeccable fashion. Detailed drawings, photographs and other records have been made, and correlated with the specimens recovered. To our best knowledge, this is the first and only wreck in Florida to have been properly investigated, scientifically speaking.

"This company is apparently the only one to attempt to fairly meet their contractual obligations under a salvage lease."

Such praise from a professional archaeologist was not easy to come by. Dr. Sears was later instrumental in gaining cabinet approval for the salvagers' six-year lease extension. Unfortunately, this apparent harmony was not destined to be long lived.

By the end of the summer of 1962, the salvagers had found countless pieces of broken pottery, numerous ship's spikes, silver buckles, twenty cannon scattered over the area and a few thousand pieces of eight. Then, the single most valuable find of all was made before the end of the year. The only trouble was, no one knew where the item had originated, and there was some question where it was found. Wagner's version of the event sounds convincing.

He said that when they wrapped up their diving season in 1962, there was little expectation of finding any more treasure until the weather became fair and the waters cleared again the next spring. Wagner therefore went back to his old habit of prowling the beach with his metal detector, hoping to pick up a few stray coins. One November day, his nineteen-year-old nephew, Rex Stocker, accompanied him on one of his beachcombing trips.

It was just after a strong northeaster had passed, and Wagner reasoned that their chances of finding something were good. He immediately set to work along the water's edge, with his battery bag slung over his shoulder, his earphones on his head and his long-handled, stove-lid-shaped sensor moving just ahead of him like a dog straining at its leash.

Periodically, as the morning wore on, the detector hummed and Wagner stopped to dig. Sometimes he found a bottle cap, sometimes a rusty tin can. But once in a while it was a rectangular piece of eight. Wagner said he began finding them so often that he lost track of time. Lacking a metal detector, Stocker grew restless and began to range well above the tide mark, where Wagner felt sure there were no coins. For the moment, he forgot his nephew as he went on searching.

Suddenly he heard the boy shout. He looked up as the youth came running toward him excitedly with something yellow draped over his arm. Wagner said his first thought was that his nephew had caught a small snake. Then, when he saw what it really was, he could not believe his eyes. It was a long, thin gold chain attached to an unusual gold pendant. Stocker said he had found it up near the bluffs, lying exposed on the sand as if it had been flung there by storm waves.

They hurried home and examined it carefully under a magnifying glass. The finely wrought chain was 11 feet 4 1/4 inches long, each link faceted with tiny floral patterns later identified as olive blossoms. The 3-inch gold pendant was shaped like a dragon, with carefully detailed scales running the length of its body. When Wagner blew into its half-opened mouth, it produced a shrill whistle. Part of the dragon's back swiveled out to make a curved toothpick. Its slender tail was shaped into a small spoon, possibly for cleaning wax out of one's ears.

Wagner had the necklace examined by experts. No one had ever seen anything like it before, nor could anyone guess its age or origin. Various museums appraised it at between $40,000 and $60,000. Stocker relinquished his find to the treasure hunters in exchange for forty shares of stock in the company.

There were only two small notes of dissent. Lou Ullian, one of Real Eight's head divers, said that the dragon pendant had not been found on the beach but had in fact been recovered from the wreck. [Mel Fisher told author Burgess the same thing in 1972.] And a chart on which the company marked the location of all its finds from the underwater site showed that the dragon pendant had been found in the wreck.

What difference did it make?

About $12,500 worth.

Here is the reason: In the United States, the common law of treasure-trove states that if something of value, defined as treasure, is found on land, it is finders-keepers. However, if that treasure is found offshore on a state's submerged land, then it is a different story. According to Florida's salvage agreement with Real Eight, the state was legally entitled to 25 percent of any such find.

The point, however, was never argued. Officially, Stocker's find was considered treasure-trove. Real Eight later sold the dragon pendant at a New York auction for $50,000.

Chapter 12

Four Fathoms to El Dorado

The salvagers bought a small cabin on the beach near the wreck site and used it as a base of operations. From then on they referred to their valuable offshore property as the "Cabin Wreck." They could have as easily called it the "Silver Wreck," since it had not yet produced any gold, only pieces of eight and artifacts, 25 percent of which was retained by the state as agreed upon in the salvage lease with Florida.

The 1963 season started slowly for the divers, who in the first four months were finding only a nominal number of single silver coins. But the returns rapidly picked up in June with the discovery of more clusters of coins. The first weighed seventy pounds and contained about 1,400 pieces of eight corroded together into a solid mass. Everyone considered the find an omen of good luck. A few days later, in a six-foot-wide area beside a shellrock ledge, they unearthed five more valuable conglomerates weighing between fifty and seventy-five pounds each and increasing their silver hoard by several thousand more coins. Before the day was out, one of the divers had found a silver crucifix encrusted with rainbow-hued shell fragments.

The quantity and frequency of these finds sparked renewed interest among the members of the group who might not normally work the bottom together. The following weekend everyone turned out, anxious to go down to see what could be found.

Minutes after The Hungry Beast started consuming its usual diet of sand, the pipe suddenly burrowed through a layer of gray clay into a concentration of broken blue and white porcelain. This in itself was not unusual, since fragments of the K'ang Hsi china were common on the site. Higgs reported finding them at the old Spanish camp in 1941, and Wagner knew from his translation of the fleet's manifest lists that the Flota vessels had carried shipments of china. But it was what lay immediately under the fragments that surprised the searchers. They began finding larger pieces. First, half a cup; then, a little farther, its other half. Below that lay a complete cup and a bowl. Then as the sand disappeared up the dredge pipe, there gradually appeared horizontal rows of cups and bowls in perfect condition, exactly as they had been stacked in the ship's hold 250 years earlier. Somehow these fragile pieces had withstood for centuries the cataclysmic destruction of the ship and the ravages of time.

The intact china so astounded the divers that they simply stared at their unique find, forgetting the wallowing sand dredge. Abruptly they were snapped out of their reverie by a loud clattering from the dredge.

Horrified, they saw that the unattended Beast was gobbling up whole cups and bowls of invaluable china, rapidly reducing it to fragments that rattled through its long aluminum alimentary canal. Hastily diverting the dredge's voracious maw, the divers rescued the remaining delicate china with careful hands.

They reported that they had found three distinct patterns of china: all white; a blue design on white; and a black enamel with faint gold border decoration. Wagner said in his book that he thought Dr. Kelso first learned of the porcelain in an obscure 1942 Florida historical quarterly. This of course was the Higgs site report. Higgs had identified similar fragments as having come from the K'ang Hsi period (1662-1722). Kelso and Wagner also knew from the old documents that much of it had been recovered by the Spanish salvagers and shipped back to Spain a year after the disaster. Correspondence with a noted authority on the porcelain revealed that at the time of its manufacture it was considered fairly common and inexpensive china destined for sale in Spain. The same china today, however, said the authority, was worth about twenty to twenty-five dollars for a large fragment, more for unbroken cups or bowls. Several museums considered it priceless. For the moment, however, the salvagers were not interested in selling their find. They hoped to keep most of their treasure intact, because the Real Eight members intended to establish a treasure museum.

Not long after finding the porcelain, one of the divers was inspecting a cannon on the bottom when he glimpsed a faint gleam beside its muzzle. Excitedly he fanned away the sand and saw several links of a finely wrought gold chain. Carefully he removed it from beneath the cannon. It was another long necklace containing a pendant that once had miniature oil paintings on its faces. Unfortunately, after its long submersion, only faint tracings of the oil paint remained.

Except for the jewelry, the Cabin Wreck had still not yielded any other gold. Where, wondered Wagner, were the doubloons? Certainly the early Spanish salvagers and the pirates that had worked the wreck had overlooked at least some of them. Were they really working the flagship of the fleet, the one which supposedly carried so much gold and silver? Or was this another ship of the fleet that had carried no gold? It was a strong temptation to let the Cabin Wreck rest while the salvagers investigated some of the other sites Wagner had learned about along the coast. But while the silver kept coming in, he reasoned, why risk valuable time and money elsewhere? After all, he felt, they had hardly scratched the surface of the Cabin Wreck yet. Real Eight stuck with this decision, and before midsummer the group's efforts were rewarded with something more than silver and artifacts.

One day Del Long and Dan Thompson were guiding The Beast over new grazing grounds in nine feet of water when the sand suddenly turned yellow with doubloons. Thompson shouted excitedly into his mouthpiece, and Long streaked for the surface, yelling and waving to the others on shore. Within minutes all were on the bottom, where they formed a circle around the site and swam toward the center of it, picking up doubloons as they went.

Wagner reported that the search turned up twenty-three 4- and 8-escudo gold coins that gleamed as brightly as they had the day they were minted. Before it was over, Long added frosting to the cake by finding a gold ring with an expansion band. As the dredge burrowed a cone-shaped hole in the bottom, Long glimpsed the ring tumbling in slow motion down the sloping sand wall. With perfect timing he thrust out his hand and let it slide onto his little finger.

The gold was a taste of what was to come. Surprisingly, few people outside Real Eight realized what the salvagers — most of whom still retained their regular jobs — had been finding on their weekend treasure-hunting trips. When the Sampan and its crew returned to Sebastian Inlet after a day over the wreck, someone around the dock always asked if they had found their pot of gold yet. The usual reply was that they had not, but that they were still looking. Then the divers transferred their sacks of silver coins from the boat to their car without elaborating on the subject.

In 1962 one of the Real Eight members, Lou Ullian, stopped by a dive shop in Los Angeles to look over new equipment. The owner was Mel Fisher, a tall, lean, balding man renowned for his treasure-hunting adventures in various parts of the world. Fisher had never found any gold, but he had an old Spanish silver coin on display that sparked a conversation between the two men. Before it was over, the West Coast treasure hunter had learned about the Florida find and was most interested. A few months later Fisher passed through Florida on his way to the West Indies with an expedition searching for Sir William Phips's fabled Silver Shoals Wreck, believed lost on reefs just north of the

Dominican Republic. He stopped to see Wagner, and they talked treasure for hours. He was most impressed by the coins Wagner showed him.

In March 1963, after an unsuccessful treasure hunt on the Shoals, Fisher visited Wagner again, this time with a proposal. He pointed out that Real Eight had more wreck sites than it could work in a lifetime. To spread the work and speed the returns, Fisher offered to bring a group of professional treasure hunters from California to work the other wrecks, splitting any new finds fifty-fifty with Real Eight after division with the state. If the group found nothing, it would get nothing for its efforts.

The idea appealed to Wagner and the other Real Eight members. While details were being worked out, Fisher returned to California, gathered his professionals into a company called Universal Salvage and took them back to Florida, ready to go. He and his attractive wife, Dolores, had sold their West Coast boat, business and home to finance the venture. The group had agreed to work Real Eight's sites for a year without pay. If by the end of that time nothing had turned up, they would call it quits and write the venture off as another unfortunate expedition.

The five men Fisher took with him came from a variety of backgrounds, but their common bond was a hunger for treasure. And they were a talented lot. Rupert Gates, Fisher's second-in- command, was a Stanford graduate with diving credits ranging from the gold-bearing rivers of the western United States to the Mediterranean to Lake Guatavita high in the Andes Mountains of South America. Panamanian-born Demosthenes Molinar, better known as "Moe," was a diesel mechanic turned diver. Jack-of-all- trades Dick Williams had been a railroad diesel engineer, welder, radio operator and electronics repairman. Walt Holzworth was a Pennsylvania Dutch farmer who had moved to California, caught the coin-collecting bug and found himself irresistibly attracted to full-time treasure hunting. Fay Field, an electronics genius, had a hobby to thank for his presence in the group. Field and his wife were avid collectors of the handsome shell of *Spondylus Americanus*, the rare spiny oyster that often inhabits old iron shipwrecks. To find his specimens, Field had to devise a quick way to find shipwrecks. He built a proton magnetometer, a supersensitive instrument that detects deviations in the earth's magnetic field caused by concentrations of iron, as in anchors, cannon, ships' fittings, etc. Fisher immediately saw its application to treasure hunting and persuaded Field to join the group. His electronic detector was destined to revolutionize treasure hunting.

Although the season was almost over, Wagner took Fisher's eager divers to the Wedge Wreck off Fort Pierce to let them test the magnetometer and familiarize themselves with the picked-over wreck where Real Eight had found the silver wedges during their initial work in 1960. No one expected to find anything at the heavily worked site, but Fisher's group got busy with a sand dredge and surprised everyone by uncovering several miniature clay animals and another silver wedge.

Despite increasingly bad weather, the next stop for the salvagers was a site just south of Vero Beach called the Sand Point Wreck. Local divers knew about this wreck at least as early as World War II, when the father of Florida treasure hunters, Art McKee, owner of the McKee Treasure Museum on Plantation Key, salvaged numerous cannon from it and sold them for scrap during the war.

Apparently, however, the site had not been worked seriously for treasure because Fisher and his men found between 1,200 and 1,500 silver coins and three gold doubloons in a few days. Unfortunately, corrosion had so badly deteriorated most of the pieces of eight that few were recognizable as coins. The heavily sulphided wafers of silver were hardly worth cheering about, but in accordance with their agreement Real Eight received half of the find.

For Fisher and his hard-bitten crew it was a long, lean

winter. Repeatedly the divers tried to work the wrecks, but the rampaging surf always drove them back. During one attempt, Fisher was slammed against the boat's bulkhead and suffered two cracked ribs. Wagner's men remembered how hard it had been for them during their first year on the Wedge Wreck and tried to bolster the California divers' morale, promising that if they could just last until spring, the reward would be worth it.

No one, in his wildest imaginings, could have guessed just how much that reward would prove to be worth for Fisher's men a few months later. But the fates that were about to guide them to a bonanza had paved the way several years before. The key figures in this historic event were three young men: Bruce Ward, Don Neiman and Frank Allen.

Bruce Ward was a midwesterner from Illinois who had come to Vero Beach in 1955. An active skin diver, he was soon influenced by the local legends of lost treasure and began looking for it at every opportunity. He combed the beach or searched the bottom offshore, using face mask, snorkel and fins and depositing his wreck fragments and artifacts in a peach basket encircled by an innertube on the surface. The more he found, the more treasure hunting intrigued him. He finally quit his job and went to work as a night watchman so that he could devote more daylight hours to his search. One day Ward struck up a friendship with another beachcomber, Don Neiman of Fort Pierce, who hunted fossils and Indian artifacts. Sharing a common interest, they decided to work together. Shortly afterward, just south of Fort Pierce, Neiman found a perfect 8-escudo gold doubloon on the beach. The two jumped for joy. Concentrating their search in that area rewarded them with a few more gold and silver coins. It was enough to make them believe they were onto something hot. Treasure was either close by or not far away, but they needed equipment and financial help to launch any serious attempt to find it.

At this point, Frank Allen of Orlando came to their aid.

Allen was a history teacher whose hobby was coin collecting. After seeing Neiman and Ward's coins and hearing their story, he agreed to invest some money in their treasure-hunting venture in exchange for a third of everything they found.

The three formed a company called The Associates. Unaware of the Real Eight lease or of the state laws governing such things, the trio purchased a fourteen-foot boat and diving equipment and went into the treasure-salvage business.

They combed the beach and dived offshore. Their efforts produced a few more coins but nothing as substantial as they had hoped. Obviously they were near a shipwreck, but it soon became apparent that this particular wreck was so badly scattered that about all they could tell about it was that there were objects from a ship on the bottom. The exact location of any concentrated treasure was a mystery they could not solve. They needed more men and better salvage equipment — necessities they could not afford. The three men were forced to make a decision.

They knew about Wagner's work on his sites and that Real Eight had the necessary men and machinery. The question was whether The Associates could reveal to them what they had found, in exchange for a piece of the action.

One August evening in 1963, Ward, Neiman and Allen visited Wagner's home and asked if they could talk with him about some treasure they had found. When he saw their bright gold coins dated 1714 and 1715, Wagner knew that the doubloons had come from the same fleet Real Eight was working.

Understandably the men were vague about the exact location of their find, but they indicated that they were willing to bargain. Wagner learned enough to be convinced that they had indeed stumbled onto something significant.

He called a meeting of the company directors, and several days later Real Eight drew up an agreement with The Associates. After the state had selected its 25 percent, the rest would be divided so that Real Eight could get 60 percent and The Associates 40 percent of everything found.

With the deal made. Ward marked the location of the site on a map of the coast. The Fisher team started searching for the wreck immediately, using their magnetometer. All they found was some metal debris from an old Naval airplane and some unexploded ordnance left over from World War II training held along this part of the coast. The divers combed the area, which Ward had indicated as the site of the wreck from September 1963 until January 1964; then they gave up in despair.

Fisher angrily reported to Wagner that they had not found the slightest trace of the ghost wreck and that he did not think it worth trying to go on.

Wagner understood Fisher's position. His divers were working on a percentage. If they found nothing, they got nothing. And for the last few months they had done a great deal of free work. Under the existing agreement with Ward, Neiman and Allen, even if they found something, Universal Salvage's share would be small. As Wagner saw it, the only thing that would keep Fisher's team interested in continuing the search was a change in the agreement.

The Associates were called in for consultation. Wagner explained the problem and offered them three alternatives: share in the search expenses, agree to a change in the present contract, or forget the whole affair.

After some haggling, Ward, Neiman and Allen allegedly agreed to a change in the agreement, under the terms of which Real Eight would get 90 percent and they would get 10 percent. The original letter on Real Eight stationery, with Kip Wagner's signature, was not redrawn. The new arrangement was supposedly a gentlemen's agreement sealed with a handshake.

Fisher's team returned to the site and began the search again. They trolled their magnetometer head back and forth over the ocean bottom, intently watching the instrument for the slightest indication of a concentration of metal. Months passed and they found nothing. Part of the problem was that at this time they did not use any organized search system. Then, in April, the divers found their first significant evidence of a shipwreck—a scattering of ballast rock on the bottom a half mile north of the area where they had been looking and farther out at sea. Foul weather prevented a closer examination of the site, but when conditions were more favorable a month later, Fisher moved in with a new piece of sand-moving equipment he had built. The new digging system used the salvage boat's engine and propeller to shoot a column of surface water down through a metal duct aimed at the bottom. It was affectionately nicknamed "The Mailbox" because of its resemblance to a street postbox. The funneled prop wash reached the ocean floor with such force that it could open an eight-by-ten-foot hole in loose deposits in ten minutes. Although it worked on the reverse principle of the injection dredge, which sucked up sand, the blaster ate holes in the bottom with far greater voracity than Real Eight's Hungry Beast, speeding up Universal Salvage's earth- moving capacity tenfold.

By the end of April, the divers had found about a hundred silver coins around the ballast rocks. Blasting continued until May 8, when one of the men, having moved a short distance away from the work area, was attracted by a dull gleam in the sand. He dug out two solid gold disks, each weighing about seven pounds. Fisher later sold a similar but smaller gold disk with Mexico mint marks for a reported $17,500.

Again the weather prevented an immediate return to the site. When it cleared, the water was so murky that the party could see very little. On a hunch, Fisher suggested moving out farther and punching a hole with The Mailbox. Since luck had favored such intuitions before, they shifted their operations to the east and dug another hole. For two days they found nothing; then, on May 24, they hit it big.

The Mailbox had just opened a deep trench down a ridge

between two rocks. Suddenly the divers saw a sight few people have ever seen. The six-foot-wide, fifteen-foot-long cavity glowed yellow with a carpet of gold coins.

Spellbound, they stared at the incredible glory hole they had uncovered; then, like fevered prospectors snatching nuggets from a fresh vein, they began grabbing coins left and right. Rather than chance letting any of the heavy gold slip through their eager fingers and fall back to the bottom to be lost again, each of the divers crammed the coins inside a glove he wore on his left hand. When a diver's glove was filled, he grabbed another fistful in his bare hand and surfaced to unload his find on the boat.

Up and down they went all day long, no one stopping for coffee or lunch. They kept picking coins off the bottom until their arms ached and their wrists were chafed raw from shoving coins into the cuffs of their gloves. But by day's end they had collected 1,033 gold coins. It was the biggest haul that they or, for that matter, any other 20th-century salvager had ever made in Florida.

Their first day's find was so large that Wagner was half afraid to see it continue at that rate for fear it would seriously affect the value of gold doubloons on the world coin market. But he need not have worried. Though their glory hole yielded 900 coins the next day, after that it grew less generous. In a week they had found nearly 2,500 doubloons before the source finally ran dry and they were forced to look elsewhere.

Wagner and Kelso supposed they had found the contents of one chest of gold, practically intact where it had dropped from the ship's disintegrating hull. Surely there were other chests nearby.

The Cabin Wreck was allowed to rest while the salvagers concentrated on the more valuable Fort Pierce gold wreck, which they now called the Colored Beach Wreck. Although the divers continued to turn up a trickle of gold coins, it was nothing compared to their first remarkable strike.

Fearing that news of their finds would attract swarms of

pirate divers, Fisher and the others took elaborate precautions to conceal the success of their salvage activities — depositing their treasure in several Fort Pierce Banks and keeping their mouths shut. In fact, their secretiveness about their discovery was one of the things that caused the first trouble between the salvagers and the state.

Chapter 13

Treasure and the State

A seemingly minor but important change occurred in 1963 that was to have considerable effect on the relationship between the treasure hunters and the state. Van Ferguson, with whom the treasure hunters had worked so well, retired as director of the Internal Improvement Fund. He was succeeded by William Kidd, a capable and conscientious man who would soon be nicknamed "Captain Kidd." Since Dr. Goggin had died in 1962, Dr. Sears was handling all the state's negotiations with the treasure hunters. Through the transition in directors of the Internal Improvement Fund, Real Eight continued as before, maintaining its communication with the state exclusively with Dr. Sears.

When, in early 1964, Mel Fisher's group found gold on the wreck south of Fort Pierce, Wagner informed Dr. Sears by telephone that the find would be put into local bank vaults until it could be divided with the state. Sears agreed and acknowledged the arrangement in a return letter. Unfortunately, this information never reached Tallahassee and William Kidd, the new director of the Internal Improvement Fund. Rumors began to fly, and Kidd did not like what he heard. It appeared to him that some company other than Real Eight, which his agency had granted a salvage lease, had found a sizable quantity of treasure and was keeping the find a secret. Moreover, this company was reportedly putting bullion into banks as collateral for loans of operational funds.

At this point, Governor Farris Bryant's investigator, Ed Reddick of the Florida Highway Patrol, was called into the case and sent to Fort Pierce to find out what was happening.

Asking discreet questions at various marinas and businesses in that area without revealing the reason for his curiosity, Reddick learned enough to be able to inform Kidd that there was considerably more truth than fiction to the rumor that had reached Tallahassee.

Kidd responded by calling in his office manager, Paul Baldwin, and ordering him to go treasure hunting. He said he had heard that out-of-state salvagers had made a large find in the Fort Pierce-Vero Beach area, and he wanted Reddick and Baldwin to learn whether or not it was covered by state leases.

Reddick was later accused by the salvagers of employing more disguises than Lon Chaney in his effort to get to the bottom of the situation. Sporting a beard, the governor's investigator appeared one day on a sailboat moored close to Fisher's salvage boat, the Dee-Gee. With a case of beer clearly in evidence in the stern of the sailboat, Reddick struck up a friendly conversation with one of the divers on the Dee-Gee. Presently he was invited aboard, with his case of beer, to see their operations. In the ensuing good cheer that developed in the stern of the salvage boat, no one apparently noticed that the bearded stranger nursed one beer through the whole occasion while he asked seemingly innocent but probing questions about their activities as treasure hunters. As a result, Reddick learned what the group was, what the men were doing in the area and generally how successful they had been.

Not everyone was that cooperative. Baldwin reported later: "We ran into a blank wall everywhere except at three banks—two in Vero Beach and one in Melbourne where some of the treasure had been deposited." Other treasure items were found in the salvagers' homes.

Finally, Reddick and Baldwin went to Wagner with their findings. They said they had evidence that Universal Salvage had been poaching on Real Eight's lease, and they were about to arrest the members of the company.

Wagner explained that Fisher's team was associated with Real Eight and that as far as he knew no laws had been broken.

He was right, but Real Eight had gone considerably beyond the bounds of its lease in subletting to Universal Salvage. As a result, Mel Fisher's group was salvaging a shipwreck owned by the state of Florida, ignorant of the state laws, rules and regulations governing such an activity. Therefore, in the eyes of the state, Universal Salvage was involved in an illegal activity.

When Reddick and Baldwin confronted Mel Fisher, he told them that he had given forty-six gold coins to his crewmen as a bonus. (All lease agreements with the state specify that "no disposition shall be made of any material recovered" without approval of the state.) One night a short while later, Captain Reddick visited the salvagers' homes and told the treasure hunters to report at once to the sheriff's office at Fort Pierce to be fingerprinted for identification cards. It was after midnight before the fingerprint man showed up. While the incident was embarrassing to those involved, it was entirely within Reddick's power as the governor's investigator to bring it off. The salvagers were told that the state was very much concerned about the lax operation Real Eight had conducted up to that time. No one ever got his identification card, but after the fingerprinting episode, Reddick started getting straight answers from everyone.

The three-week investigation gave rise to sensational news stories. The press generally pictured the salvagers as modern-day pirates reaping out-of-bounds sea treasure with the intention of beating the state out of a fortune. At that time the treasure recovered was erroneously reported to be worth at least a million dollars.

On June 9, Kidd wrote a letter to Colonel H. N. Kirkman, head of the state highway patrol, commending Captain Reddick for his part in the investigation. "This is to advise you," said the Internal Improvement Fund director, "that Capt. Reddick and a representative of this office have during the last week located sizable recoveries of gold and silver, which have been removed from state-owned property. They are now in the process of inventorying and collecting all of this material and storing it in a safe location. . . .

"Let me say," Kidd continued, "that through the efforts of Ed [Reddick] I believe that the state of Florida will recover two or three hundred thousand dollars that otherwise would have been lost. …At the appropriate time I will bring this matter to the attention of the cabinet."

Apparently the moment never arrived, because the subject was never mentioned at a public cabinet meeting.

In early June, while Reddick and Baldwin were busy inventorying the treasure from Fisher's Fort Pierce find, and the newspapers were playing up the angle that Florida was getting the worst of the deal in its arrangement with treasure hunters, the Internal Improvement Fund hired someone to look after the state's underwater archaeological interests. He was Carl Clausen, a marine archaeologist with a master's degree from the University of Florida. On recommendations that included Dr. Sears's, Kidd had got in touch with him in Gainesville and asked if he would accept the job of trying to oversee what was going on. Clausen accepted, and the governor's cabinet appointed him the archaeologist to supervise the activities of the salvage contractors.

Not only was this a new position for the recent graduate, but no one in Tallahassee, certainly not Clausen himself, had much of an idea what the job would entail. He was green, but he was not an innocent. He had been well trained professionally by Dr. Goggin, and he was well acquainted with the realm in which he was to work. Though born in Texas, Clausen had been raised in Bradenton on Florida's west coast. As a twelve-year-old in 1949, he was skin diving and spearfishing when the sport was so new that all of his equipment was homemade.

When Clausen found he had been hired to do a job nobody understood, his first request was for over five hundred dollars' worth of diving equipment so that he could get down and see for himself what was happening on the wreck sites.

About mid-June he flew to Fort Pierce with William Kidd and Assistant Attorney General Kenneth Ballenger to meet Paul Baldwin, who was helping Captain Reddick complete his investigation. The idea was to familiarize Clausen with the people and the situations involved. Then came the opportunity for the new archaeologist to visit the treasure site and see the salvagers in action.

Everyone motored out in Fisher's salvage boat, the Dee-Gee. The treasure hunters were tense and uneasy with the state people aboard. While the divers suited up, they kept glancing at the archaeologist to see, he imagined, if he knew which end to buckle his weight belt on. Then, instead of revealing what was at that time considered their secret equipment — the blaster — they put over their injection dredges and took the state people down to use them. Clausen was with one of Universal Salvage's best divers, Walt Holzworth, the friendly Pennsylvania Dutchman. Clausen had worked with air lifts before, and the operation of the injection dredge was not much different. As he burrowed down through the sand with the device, out tumbled a small 1-real silver coin about the size of a thumbnail. The archaeologist picked it up and showed it to Holzworth. The treasure hunter stared at Clausen's find, then did a strange thing. He took the coin and scratched it against the side of the dredge!

Clausen learned later that the treasure hunters had purposely put the state people far from the wreck site simply to give them a taste of the procedure. His turning up a coin where none was supposed to have been was the reason for Holzworth's odd reaction.

As soon as the press began printing stories suggesting that the treasure hunters had been taking advantage of the state by seemingly unfair divisions in which Florida got ships' spikes and ceramic sherds—so-called archaeological junk—while the salvagers reaped the real treasure, the state took a closer look at their program. A special advisory committee was set up to examine Florida's relationship with treasure hunters. Out of the chaos several things became clear: 1) For more than three years private salvagers had operated without any direct and continuous supervision from the state. As a result, efforts to audit their books with any accuracy were futile. 2) The policing of salvage operations was so lax that the state learned about the discoveries only by rumor and subsequent investigation by a highway patrol captain. 3) If it had adhered to the letter of the law. Real Eight had no legal right to salvage the Fort Pierce treasure—it had not obtained a pinpoint salvage lease on that wreck site. 4) Until Clausen was hired, the state had no full-time employees to monitor salvage or to oversee the division of treasure and artifacts.

The immediate reaction to all this was to sway judgment too far in the opposite direction. Lacking first-hand experience in the type of commercial salvage operation that Universal Salvage Inc. was mounting for Real Eight on the wrecks, Dr. Charles Fairbanks, chairman of the salvage advisory committee, announced that the state should get100 percent of the finds and that the locations of all artifacts recovered from the wrecks should be recorded to "the nearest inch" by the salvagers. Dr. Hale Smith, chairman of the Department of Anthropology at Florida State University, the man who had scientifically investigated the Higgs site and was told of the wreck location just offshore, said that the state could have pinpointed and recovered the materials by itself.

Wagner was extremely concerned about the situation because the adverse publicity was driving a wedge between the salvagers and the state. After the initial investigation, Reddick's analysis was that the Real Eight Company could not do the salvage work while Fisher's group, Universal Salvage, could do and was doing it. At that point, William Kidd was on the verge of breaking Wagner's lease over the Colored Beach Wreck incident, with the intention of giving to Mel Fisher the legal rights to salvage the wrecks. If things did not get straightened out in a hurry, Wagner knew he could lose everything he had worked for.

He and Fisher went to Tallahassee to see if they could iron out some of the difficulties with Kidd, but they accomplished nothing. Shortly afterward another attempt was made, this time by several other representatives from Real Eight. Kidd was too busy to see them, so they requested and got an audience with Governor Bryant. After they had explained the whole story to him, then to the attorney general, Jimmy Kynes, the governor asked Kidd to work out a mutually agreeable arrangement with the salvagers.

As a result, an agreement was reached between Real Eight and the state in which the salvagers relinquished their exclusive right to explore the fifty-mile area from Sebastian to Stuart, making it possible for other salvage companies to have leases in the area. In exchange, they received pinpoint salvage leases on the eight wreck sites that the company thought were associated with the 1715 fleet.

After that, except for an occasional flare-up, most of the fireworks died down. The salvagers continued work on the Colored Beach Wreck, but now Clausen accompanied them in an attempt to record some of the archaeological information from the wreck.

Unfortunately, this was not the most ideal situation for either the treasure hunters or the archaeologist. Time was valuable to the salvagers. Any delays to recover artifacts of little monetary value to them were costly. In the circumstances, however, both parties tried to make the best of it. Clausen would try to chart the locations of important artifacts, while the salvagers would periodically pause in their search for treasure to help him haul up anything he could not handle alone. To make matters worse, the wreck was a nightmare. Thanks to the fury of the initial hurricane that destroyed the fleet, coupled with almost two and a half centuries of other natural depredations by everything from ship worms to storm tides, the Colored Beach Wreck was scattered over ten acres of ocean bottom and covered with sand. The site was approximately three nautical miles south of old Fort Pierce Inlet. It lay some 500 to 1,500 feet offshore in eight to twenty feet of water under a white sand bottom punctuated with occasional outcroppings of Anastasia limestone and beds of shell or coquina rock. Wide grooves in the limestone running generally parallel to the beach were filled with sand, varying in depth from several inches to more than five feet. Constant wave action in the area kept the bottom constantly stirred up so that even on a good day maximum visibility was about eighteen inches.

Fisher's fifty-foot Navy launch, the Dee-Gee, served as a base of operations. Since the team had had such good luck with their blaster, they relied on it almost entirely for all their excavating. In the beginning there was no set pattern in where they dug. They blasted holes in the bottom wherever intuition directed. It was a haphazard method that sometimes resulted in the salvagers' working areas they had already searched. Now, however, to keep track of new finds, they established a grid system. The east-west base line, or axis, was a length of 3/8-inch chain laid across the bottom between the cascabels of two cannon. A second chain bisected it at right angles in a north-south direction through the cascabel of a shoreward cannon. As work continued out from these base lines, additional lengths of chain would be placed parallel to them at twenty-five-foot intervals.

It was a glamorless, grueling routine. The men would get up at 5:30 each morning and be at the site aboard the Dee-Gee at seven o'clock. If the waves were not too bad, the salvage boat would be positioned with three anchors, one off the bow and two off the stern, to keep it from shifting around the site while the excavating went on. The blaster was cranked up, sending its invisible column of water down to the bottom, where it began eating a hole. Divers hovered around the edges of the rapidly growing pit watching intently for whatever might appear. Coins, glassware, pottery sherds, unidentifiable sand-encrusted metal conglomerates and anything even vaguely resembling an artifact were quickly snatched up and deposited in a collecting bag. As the pit deepened, the loose sloping sand walls crept higher, and the divers looked as if they were scratching around in the bottom of a giant ant lion's trap. If something too large to handle appeared in the blue-green world of swirling water and sand, the blaster was shut off until some adequate means was found to raise the item without damaging it. On days of little current, the sand and mud settled back down on the site, creating an eerie gloom around the divers.

With each find, Clausen carefully measured its distance from a chain, shot an azimuth of its position from the boat, and noted the information on a graph chart of the site. This procedure was repeated at each new excavation. The Dee-Gee was repositioned by hauling in or letting out on the three anchor lines; then the blaster commenced again. One afternoon while searching among ballast rock, Fisher discovered an object he thought was a waterlogged piece of timber. Instead of being wood, however, the object turned out to be a thirty-five-pound silver bar camouflaged by incrustations.

Clausen had no control over where or how the treasure hunters worked. If they moved too fast for him, he was often left hauling chains and making measurements by himself. Normally he spent six to ten hours a day underwater, surfacing only long enough to grab a bite to eat and to change air tanks. At night there were the artifacts to catalog and care for. The salvagers worked a minimum of sixteen hours a day, twenty to thirty days a month, throughout the diving season, which ended abruptly in late August when two hurricanes— Cleo and Dora—blew in from the Atlantic and put an end to things.

It had been a good year for the salvagers. Clausen had spot-excavated approximately a two-acre square of the ten-acre site. Almost all the wreck material, except the cannon and ballast rock, was removed. Of the five cannon they found, Clausen carefully measured and examined two of them underwater. Almost eight feet long, they were muzzle-loading, smooth-bore weapons typical of the period and capable of firing a variety of projectiles. One still contained a wooden tampion (moisture and dust plug) wedged in its bore. The salvaged artifacts included cannon balls, round shot, bar-shot (two 6- to 9-pound projectiles joined by an iron bar which when fired from a small cannon wreaked havoc among the masts and rigging of another ship), pistol and musket balls, a heavily encrusted sword handle, pottery sherds, four pairs of brass navigational dividers, sounding leads, a pewter plate, lead patches and window cames, wrecking bars, deadeyes and miscellaneous ship fastenings. The treasure items included several silver knives, forks and spoons, parts of 2 silver candlesticks, 8 pieces of gold chain, 1 silver bar, 6 silver and gold ingots, 16 gold rings, more than 3,700 gold coins and 200 pounds of silver coins.

When the division date for this treasure finally arrived, representatives of the state—a certified public accountant, Captain Ed Reddick, Paul Baldwin and Clausen—met with officials of Real Eight and Universal Salvage at a Vero Beach bank to divide the finds. The problem was that no one there was fully trained and qualified to select artifacts, neither the state representatives nor the salvagers. Clausen was the only one who had any qualifications for identifying, analyzing and determining the scientific value of artifacts, but since he had just come on the scene, he was unsure of his power to affect the situation.

The salvagers took the initiative and tried to make the division as fair as possible by breaking down the treasure into four equal lots. For example, all the coins were stacked in fours according to their dates, denominations and condition;

the jewelry and other valuables were stacked in four separate but equal piles along with the artifacts. To a layman this might seem like the easiest and most logical way to make a division. And it might have been if these items had been anything other than 250-year-old artifacts with individual values. A qualified archaeologist should have been on hand to evaluate all the materials, categorize them, inventory them, and then make the selection for the state on the basis of their scientific and historical value to the people of Florida.

When Clausen realized that, instead, the division was to be the random choice of a layman, and that there was really nothing he could do about it, he left the bank in disgust. He could not conceive of a more illogical way to divide such artifacts.

The state's "share" was then selected by the highway patrolman, Captain Ed Reddick, who chose which of the four stacks of coins he felt he wanted. He did the same with the four piles of valuables.

In the circumstances, everyone present thought this the best and fairest way of dividing the treasure. Others, however, felt differently. Dr. Charles Fairbanks, chairman of the state advisory committee, reacted quickly with stinging but justified criticism. In a letter to Kidd, he said:

"Dr. Dickinson and I noted that [after Clausen left] no archaeologist or historian was present to make an evaluation of these unique items that could not be divided on a numerical basis. In one case the state apparently received an 8-escudo gold coin as its share of a lot, which included a large bell and a holy medallion. Both the bell and the medallion have a research value far beyond the nominal value of the coin.

"In such cases," said Fairbanks, "an archaeologist or historian from the committee should be present whenever divisions are made to protect the historic values involved."

Such a situation was not to occur again.

Although he later put together what was to be the first bona fide site report on a shipwreck ever published by a professional archaeologist in the United States, Clausen was disappointed with the meager attempt at archaeological work made on the Colored Beach Wreck. He was more than ever convinced that commercial treasure hunting and underwater archaeology simply did not mix. If a treasure hunter and an archaeologist found a plank on a shipwreck, for example, the archaeologist would try to determine what relationship that plank bore to the ship, observing details, drawing or photographing it in place. The salvager would only be interested in lifting the plank to see if there might be a gold coin under it.

The experiences of that first summer were enough to make Clausen realize that there was much Florida history locked in those wrecks and that commercial salvage was not the way to preserve it.

Small gold bee contains an emerald.

Gold ring with emeralds.

Decorated brass snuff box.

Ship silverware with mint marks.

Gold finger ingot with official stamps.

Marine encrustations on a sword hilt.

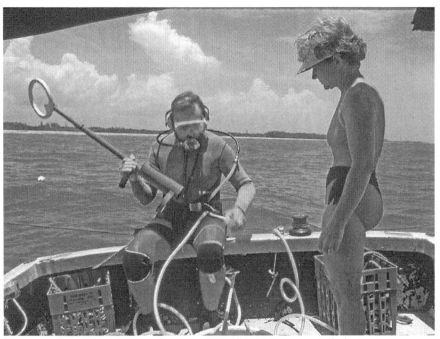

Bob Weller prepares to search with a metal detector.

Treasure divers gleeful about finding golden rosary.

An elegant gold and onyx beaded rosary.

Chapter 14
The Great Florida Gold Rush

William Kidd left the Internal Improvement Fund in 1964 and was replaced by Robert Parker, who inherited all the headaches associated with the job of directing Florida's salvage-lease program. Parker resented the time the salvage-lease program demanded. He tended to ignore problems and adopted a don't-rock-the-boat policy. This laissez-faire attitude toward treasure hunting made him well liked among some of the long-established salvagers. Others, however, criticized him for showing favoritism, allegedly granting salvage leases to the few while refusing the many. But one thing can be said in his favor: Parker realized that the state simply was not equipped to cope with a full-scale gold rush, and that no amount of private or political pressure was going to alter the situation.

That fall Mel Fisher moved part of his operation south to Marathon, where one of his corporations. Armada Research, had leases to search for shipwrecks. When word spread through the Keys that Fisher was invading the area with his sophisticated salvage and detection equipment, many a hard-bitten treasure hunter who had always worked independently without benefit of legal leases was up in arms. Why didn't he stay where he belonged instead of muscling in on their favorite picking grounds?

One of the strongest protests was a letter to Governor Bryant from Hugh Brown, then president of the Florida Keys Underwater Guides Association. This loosely organized group of charter-boat captains specialized in taking divers out to the reefs to dive, collect tropical fish or pick up a few artifacts from one of the known wrecks. Brown asked the governor to suspend all leases in the Keys until assurances were made that Fisher's powerful excavating dredges were not destroying shipwrecks that were tourist attractions. Brown pointed out that the underwater guides depended on these wrecks for their livelihood, since they took visitors to see them. One wreck had already been destroyed, he said, and eight others had been damaged by treasure salvagers. Apart from their churning up the wrecks with their air lifts, just what kind of damage the treasure hunters were causing that some of the diving charter captains were not, was not quite clear.

Two months after Brown's letter. Internal Improvement Fund representatives Baldwin (the office manager turned investigator), Ballenger, the assistant attorney general, and Clausen called for a public meeting in Marathon to discuss the problem. Brown, representing the Florida Keys Underwater Guides Association, said that his group was not opposed to operations of the salvage firms but was concerned about whether the wrecks would remain intact, about what would be left after the salvagers got through tearing them apart.

Mel Fisher told the gathering that there were hundreds of shipwrecks in the area and that forty-nine out of fifty his firm had found were left undisturbed because his detection gear did not indicate the presence of gold or silver. "We don't destroy those shipwrecks," said Fisher. "If we detect gold or silver, we bring it up, but we don't pick up cannons or anchors or anything like that."

Incredibly, nine out of ten divers there believed Fisher actually had a device to detect gold and silver. What he really had at this time was a simple but workable homemade version of the proton magnetometer, the device capable of detecting minor but measurable variations or distortions in the earth's local magnetic field caused by large iron objects such as cannon, anchors or small clusters of the iron pins or spikes that held the old ships together.

Ballenger outlined the kinds of salvage leases granted to salvage firms, and Clausen emphasized that the archaeological value of the wrecks was lost when they were picked over and the artifacts removed indiscriminately — whether by treasure hunters or customers of the Underwater Guides Association.

Parker was telephoned a report of the hearing, in which Brown asserted that he was perfectly in accord with the way the salvagers said they were handling the wrecks. Still, there was growing suspicion in Tallahassee that tourists were being allowed to take souvenirs from the wrecks, that in fact this was perhaps one of the lures guides held out to the adventuresome tourist — a chance to go on a "treasure hunt." Moreover, there were even rumors that the guides may have salted the wrecks a little, dropping a few trinkets here and there for customers to find.

The state's special advisory committee recommended that Florida begin a program of underwater investigations and archaeological research on the wrecks in public waters. As usual, the opposition cried that the state was trying to get into treasure hunting for itself, keeping the legitimate treasure hunters out while claiming all finds for the state.

Governor Bryant's reaction was that private salvage companies could do a better job than the state because of the profit motive. "If the state is going out on its own," he said, "it will have to do the exploring as well as the salvaging. We can't wait for someone else to find the treasure and then run out and pirate it."

But how could the state pirate what according to Florida law was already hers?

The monumental misunderstanding of the situation, as reflected in the governor's statement, epitomized the problems in Tallahassee.

Meanwhile, Real Eight was confronted with a problem of its own — a lack of funds. This may sound strange considering the fortune in gold and silver the salvagers had amassed in local bank vaults. But there were bills to be paid, and until some of the treasure could be converted to cash, it was virtually useless to the finders. Converting it to cash, however, presented a problem common to all treasure hunters and diamond dealers: if the value of rare coins or gems is to be maintained, only a few can be allowed on the market at any one time. Real Eight had last disposed of some of its coins in 1961; now it was time to do it again. The salvagers chose a representative collection, including many one-of-a-kind specimens to give the offering depth. They cleaned and polished their choicest items, and that October they went to market.

Henry Christensen, a world-famous coin auctioneer and an authority on Spanish colonial issues, presented the rare collection at an auction in Hoboken, New Jersey. Most of the coins were cataloged at prices of several hundred dollars each. A few were expected to bring well over $1,000 each. The consignment of more than one hundred coins was almost entirely gold, the dates ranging from the 1600s to the early 1700s. All were minted in Mexico or South America, and none was dated later than 1714.

Response to the auction was gratifying. What the salvagers did not know, however, was that the bidders were far more knowledgeable about the offering than anyone had suspected. Without the slightest change of expression, F. Xavier Calico, an eminent collector and coin dealer from Barcelona, Spain, bought the rarest coin of the lot—a round 1695 Carlos II 8-escudo "royal" from the Mexico City mint— for $3,500. None other has ever been found on the wrecks. Another rare item in the collection, unknown to the salvagers before the bidding began, was an almost mint-perfect 4-escudo 1711 gold doubloon estimated in the catalog to be worth $2,000. It sold for $3,600. By the end of the auction, private collectors had bought most of the coins, and the salvagers were richer by $29,000.

Back in Florida, Real Eight and Fisher's company, now called Treasure Salvors, divided the loot according to their various agreements and got ready to harvest more coins. Despite the auction's apparent success, it seemed ironical that after years of hard work recovering a treasure estimated to be worth millions, the most any of the treasure hunters had realized from it was a few thousand dollars already destined to be consumed by the payment of long-overdue bills.

Through 1964, most of the Real Eight crew spent nights and weekends converting a newly purchased boat into a salvage vessel to replace their cherished but frequently unseaworthy Sampan. What started out as little more than a fifty-foot copper-sheathed shell with a thirteen-foot beam and a belch-fire engine was by year's end a freshly painted salvage boat with a reconditioned diesel engine, a fiberglassed deck, a pilothouse and steering gear. In honor of her original status she was christened the Derelict. Mounted prominently through her side abaft of midship was the pride of Real Eight's ingenious mechanics — a blaster to end all blasters.

Instead of being a square box utilizing the boat's propeller power, as Fisher's device had done, this was a quarter-ton steel cylinder eight feet long and three and a half feet wide, with its four-bladed propeller inside coupled to a 1935 Ford rear-end transmission. Three holes were cut around the cylinder to let in water, and the engine was mounted sideways on the boat. On its first trial the blaster exceeded all expectations. Wagner said it sounded like sixteen jet fighters roaring off the runway at the same time. It blew mud off the bottom of Wabasso harbor for two hundred feet or more. It blasted not only modest holes but elephantine pits. Yet it could be idled down so low that the thirty-six-inch-wide column of swirling water aimed at the bottom became gentle enough to fan sand off a fragile artifact without injuring it. This "Big Bertha" of underwater excavators would soon prove itself in a spectacular debut performance, but not before the state began tightening its salvage program.

In January 1965, Florida's new governor, Haydon Burns, placed a moratorium on all new treasure-salvage leases until he could appraise the situation and determine how the state's position might be improved. Almost all of this evaluation apparently took place in the governor's office. He did, however, come out strongly in opposition to the state's going into the "treasure-salvage business" because he felt it would be too expensive. Finally he called for a program with stronger controls. In response, the state legislature created an Antiquities Commission staffed with state archaeologists, historians, anthropologists, museum curators, geologists and members of the Florida Board of Conservation. These persons were to advise and assist the governor and his cabinet in matters pertaining to the recovery, restoration and protection of all objects covered by Florida's antiquities law, including historic sites, fossil deposits, rare documents and treasure-trove. For administrative purposes the new commission was under Florida's Internal Improvement Fund; however, it would take over from Parker's staff the responsibilities of issuing salvage leases. To strengthen the program, the state hired a ten-man salvage patrol of conservation officers to observe salvage operations and guard against pirating by unlicensed treasure hunters. The Antiquities Commission was under the chairmanship of Dr. J. C. Dickinson, director of the Florida State Museum, who in his early capacity as head of the state's advisory committee was no stranger to the perplexing problems involving Florida and her treasure hunters.

As soon as possible, Clausen got the ten-man team of conservation officers out of their role of watchmen and into something more beneficial to the program. He suggested that they be put on the salvage boats to record the artifacts recovered. When the state agreed to try this plan, Clausen taught the men how to plot a boat's salvage position on a site, how to fill out field notes and forms and how to care for the artifacts brought up. Eventually the conservation officers were replaced by personnel with some training in archaeological techniques, and they in turn soon trained other technicians in specialized procedures, which program resulted in the basic system still in use.

During the moratorium only three salvage firms had legal instruments to operate: Real Eight Company, which included Fisher's group, Treasure Salvors, the Martin County Historical Society, and the Perdido Corporation. Through the early 1965 diving season, Real Eight's salvage boat, the Derelict, alternated between working the Cabin Wreck near Sebastian Inlet and the gold wreck south of Fort Pierce. On May 19, her crew made its first important find. The divers went down 500 feet north of where Fisher's team was working the original hot spot, and struck gold—nineteen doubloons the first day, several more the next week, plus a few hitherto undiscovered cannon, musket balls, pewter plates, ship fittings and two anchors. It was a proper initiation for the new vessel.

The significant distance between the two finds was further evidence of how scattered the wreck was. Apparently the ship struck with such force that she disintegrated, strewing wreckage and treasure over several acres of the bottom. This is why Ward, Neiman and Allen had been unable to pinpoint it and why it was practically anyone's guess where treasure might lie hidden beneath the camouflaging layers of sand.

Wagner said that when it came to predicting where treasure might be, Del Long was either one of the luckiest fellows around, or he was a gifted prognosticator. Not that he made a habit of predicting their good fortunes, but whenever he got "that certain prophetic feeling," the others knew from past experience that it paid to hear him out. For instance, one weekend in late May, Long said he had a feeling that they would strike gold—"right over there." He pointed out a spot about a thousand feet from where the Derelict was working.

A couple of days later when the blaster opened a hole not fifty feet from the area Long had indicated, the divers found 130 gold coins in twenty-four feet of water. That night word of the strike went out to the other team members, and the next morning everyone crowded aboard the Derelict as it motored out to the site. On station the blaster fired its low-pressure, high-volume jet of water at the bottom that opened a thirty-foot-wide pit. The divers went down, and for the second time in their career, they were stunned by the spectacle of gold coins carpeting the broad white sand depression. Some coins were stacked three and four deep.

It was the gold rush all over again. Divers grabbed coins by handfuls; they lowered buckets and filled them to the brim with doubloons. All day they worked feverishly, gathering gold, hoisting bucketfuls of the precious coins to the surface and dumping them in a golden cascade onto the deck of the Derelict. For the second time they had found an underwater El Dorado, and they made the most of it. In that one day they recovered 1,128 gold coins. Nearly half were 8-escudo coins the size of fifty-cent pieces, which from their fine condition were worth anywhere from $500 to more than $2,000 apiece.

As had happened so often in the past, the weather prevented them from returning to the site for the next few days. It was June 3 before they were able to try again, and this time they found only a few coins. Considering how many they had taken the first day, what had happened was no mystery. Once again they thought they might have stumbled onto the scattered contents of a single chest, although strangely enough no such container of coins appeared on the manifest of this ship, which was later identified as the patache of the Flota. The intensity of the salvagers' initial efforts had simply exhausted the supply of gold coins in that spot. It did not, however, exhaust the hunters' desire to find more. But by now the salvagers were not the only ones with a bad case of gold fever.

When the Fort Pierce treasure strike hit the headlines from coast to coast, the Great Florida Gold Rush was on. Gold seekers came by bus, plane, car and foot. They came in droves—amateur and professional treasure hunters, cranks, con men, crooks and the curious—all converging at the scene of the strike along Florida's southern coasts. They swarmed over the beaches between Sebastian and Wabasso, searching for coins. They shook the sleepy little towns out of their lethargy by buying every piece of scuba and skin-diving equipment local merchants had to offer. They swam or boated out to the Colored Beach Wreck in 1964 and out to the Cabin Wreck in 1965 in such numbers that Treasure Salvors and Real Eight had to shoo them away each time they went to work. They bought every copy they could find of the early version of John Potter's then out-of-print The Treasure Diver's Guide, sometimes paying up to $65 for it. The book was in such demand that the local library took its copy out of circulation and made it available for reference only. They bought so many copies of Ralph Odum's copyrighted treasure map entitled "Ye True Chart of Pirate Treasure lost or hidden in the land and waters of Florida" that its printers had to work overtime to fill their orders.

At Fort Pierce city fathers made a bid for the anticipated influx of tourist dollars by dubbing their area "The Treasure Coast." The idea was to attract travelers by circulating the fiction that beachcombing would bring Spanish coins two and a half centuries old as souvenirs.

The rush was overwhelming. The crowds came, looked and spent. Everyone in town talked of Spanish treasure. Newcomers itched to get offshore to see the bottom paved with gold. Rumors spread that new finds not only equaled but exceeded the reported $1.6 million in gold, silver and artifacts recovered by the Real Eight-Treasure Salvors combine. Stories circulated of professional treasure hunters flipping ancient coins for drinks in Fort Pierce bars. Strangers greeted citizens with such jocular queries as "How's the gold today?"

How indeed. It might not have been made in Spain, but it was rolling in. The solitary Fort Pierce coin dealer, who before the rush was doing a penny-ante business, found his trade enlarged 400 percent. Gift shops repeatedly sold out of treasure maps and charts claiming to show the "reefs" that had caused the wrecks. Marinas were doing a land-office business renting everything that would float to sightseers, and there was not an underwater guide from Fort Pierce to Key West who did not have a waiting list of customers as long as his snorkel.

Strangers stalked the beaches, their heads down, eyes scrutinizing the water's edge for gold doubloons winking in the sand like tiny suns. Some, believing that the early birds get the coins, trudged down the breaker-scoured beaches before sunup. Late arrivals had to be satisfied with searching in the dawn patrol's footprinted wake. Bottle caps and seashells were what most found. A very few actually did find coins.

As in most gold rushes, there were those who were eager to sell the searchers gadgets "guaranteed" to find gold. One such "salesman" showed up in town with a forked wand resembling a water dowser's stick, which he said would unerringly point to gold. To prove it he would gather a crowd around him he aimed the wand in the general direction of the local bank and gazed triumphantly at the stick leaping and jerking in his hands. Another operator tried to sell a magic pendulum he said would swing until it "sniffed" gold; then it would quickly line up on the precious metal. He also made a note of where the local banks were.

Meanwhile, serious treasure hunters bent on guarding their activities were unnerved by their sudden popularity. When strangers strayed too close to their bailiwicks, they went to elaborate lengths to learn their identities. "You see a man in a white shirt and tie looking for sea shells or sitting back in a thicket, and you tend to get suspicious," said one Fort Pierce man. Some of this paranoia probably stemmed from the state's investigation of the treasure hunters in 1964.

"Every gold rush has produced its crop of con men and counterfeiters, and you can be sure this one will too," prophesied Fort Pierce's News-Tribune editor, Tom Cope, long before the Florida gold rush was in full swing. "Fakers are sure to come along with wild claims, looking for sucker financing. There will be lawsuits. Legal salvors or pirates, it's the same story: of all the metals, gold is the one most likely to produce moral blood-poisoning."

Cope's copy was as true as the biblical handwriting on the wall.

The Fisher find was hardly dry before the Neiman-Ward suit hit the headlines. Then, in March 1965, part-time treasure hunter Ray Lorenz went to court to challenge the right of the state of Florida to control offshore salvage and treasure hunting. Lorenz's suit claimed that treasure salvage came under the jurisdiction of the Federal government and that the only right granted to Florida was the right to control the leasing and recovery of natural resources such as sand and gravel lying within its three-mile limit. He insisted the Federal government had granted no right to Florida to issue leases to those who desired to search for abandoned property. Lorenz's case was badly researched and prepared. The suit named as defendants Martin County Judge Mallory Johnson and the trustees of the Internal Improvement Fund, consisting of the governor and state cabinet.

Lorenz, an insurance salesman, said he had been denied a lease to hunt treasure in Martin County, a coastal county located on Florida's lower east coast. The wreck that he reportedly was interested in was supposed to be one of those lost with the 1715 fleet, although there is no support in any of the documents for any 1715 wrecks south of the Fort Pierce wreck. The lease for that area had been granted some years before to the Martin County Historical Society, and Lorenz asked the court to issue a declaratory decree saying that the state had "no right, title, claim or interest" in offshore treasure hunting. A favorable ruling for Lorenz would have thrown out state control over salvage and treasure seekers, resulting in an "open door" policy for all ocean treasure hunters. However, when the suit came up before Circuit Judge Hugh Taylor in Tallahassee, he quickly dismissed it on the grounds that the Federal government was not involved. Lorenz's argument that the shipwrecks were "abandoned property" and not natural resources, thereby making them legal to salvage, was never answered. Though to some this might have seemed a good point, society does not function on the principle of "finders-keepers, losers-weepers," whether a person's car, his money or, as in this case, his American heritage is involved. The decision of the court was a fortunate but hollow victory for the state.

Further confirmation of Cope's predictions that the Florida gold rush would attract more than tourists and publicity began in May 1965, when the St. Petersburg Times headlined a news story that seven treasure hunters claimed to have found another rich treasure cache on the wreck of a Spanish galleon they had supposedly discovered ninety miles south of St. Petersburg in the Gulf of Mexico. According to John Sykes, spokesman for the group of St. Petersburg treasure hunters calling themselves the "Lucky Seven," he and his companions (whom he would not name) had located the wreck more than a year before in water so shallow that coins could be picked up by waders. Sykes said his group had applied for a salvage permit from the state about two months before the east coast strike, but it had been held up. Now he felt sure it would be issued.

On learning of the Gulf find, Clausen flew to St. Petersburg with the state's field investigator, Philip Thibedeau, to examine and catalog the treasure. Then, in accordance with state policy, it would be kept in safe-deposit boxes at the First Federal Savings and Loan Association's office there. According to the news story, the artifacts and treasure consisted of three Aztec figurines five to six inches tall, two of gold, one of bronze; an Aztec sacrificial sword with a bronze blade and a silver hilt; and a number of coins, mostly silver pieces of eight dated 1698 and coming from the Mexico City mint.

As soon as Clausen examined the find he suspected that the items were fake. The statement that he and Philip

Thibedeau released to the press, however, said only that the state had begun an investigation to check the treasure's authenticity and that there were some points of conflict with the coins found on the east coast.

That was understatement indeed. Twenty-five pieces of eight were found to be spurious; the knight's head on the hilt of the so-called sacrificial sword was thought to have come from a Seaforth's aftershave or cologne bottle, and two of the three small statues represented as being Aztec were believed to be mail-order bookends from Mexico. In addition, hundreds of counterfeit coins similar to the forgeries were being circulated throughout Florida and the southeastern United States.

Doing some backtracking on the suspicious Gulf treasure, the St. Petersburg Times reporter learned that Sykes had shown the items to Wallace Minto, a Sarasota metallurgical expert, before the state people saw them. Minto had also suspected that the finds were not genuine. "The sword intrigued me the most," he said. "Although I didn't have an opportunity to touch it, several flaws were evident. The blade was not steel. It was either bronze or copper. They [the treasure hunters] said it was bronze. Bronze swords have not been used since the time of the Romans. It was too soft. The hilt of the sword was shaped in the form of a Teutonic cross which the Spaniards never used and the Germans have only used in modern times. The cross looked very much like a mail-order advertisement of a few years ago for an SS officer's knife."

Minto's observations on the other artifacts were equally interesting: "The figurines were not gold," he said, "but gold plated in a modem style called bright gold. They were also castings. The art of casting was not developed by the Aztecs. [Here, Minto either was incorrect or was misquoted by the newspaper.] The specific gravity was such that I believe these to be brass. The figurines themselves,

I am certain, were bookends you could buy through the

mail from Mexico a few years ago."

Closer examination of the coins revealed that they had been cast, a process the Spaniards had not used in making their early coins. Instead, they cut them from poured strips of silver, clipped them to legal weight, then stamped them between steel dies. The cast counterfeits had straight, sharp edges all around. The silver was hard rather than soft like pure Spanish silver, which can usually be marked with a fingernail. Some counterfeits also bore file marks, an unmistakable indication that the coins were bogus or at least altered. Less obvious discrepancies were found on the faces of the coins. For instance, one series of fake 8-real pieces was marked with the date 1711, but the crest or royal shield shown on the coin belonged to a period seventy-five years earlier. A bead from a portion of a decorative semicircle was missing. This could happen in genuine coins when there was a defect in the Spaniards' die—but two silver coins from the same die were seldom encountered. Yet the same defect appeared on all the fake coins in the series. Lack of symmetry and a notch in the outline of a coin's embossed shield indicated the counterfeiter's carelessness. Mint marks on the forgeries were OM, with F, the initial of the royal assayer. This was the Mexico City mint. But in 1711, the mark was OXM, and the assayer's initial was not F but J. Assayer F did not appear on the scene until several years later. In some places the counterfeits contained only meaningless marks. Unfortunately, however, the quality of the forgeries, though poor, was still good enough to fool collectors who knew little or nothing about early Spanish coins.

Authorities learned that of the several hundred other counterfeit coins already circulating, most were 8 reals, but there were others of smaller denominations. An indeterminate number of sets containing 1, 2, 4 and 8 reals had been sold to coin collectors along the "Treasure Coast," some for $140 a set. One coin dealer in Fort Pierce even tried to sell sets of the counterfeits after it had been brought to his attention that they were fakes. Considering that each set could have been manufactured for less than five dollars, it was a lucrative business.

Obviously the counterfeiters were capitalizing on the genuine find from the 1715 wrecks off the Florida east coast. Real Eight and Treasure Salvors were in no way involved with the counterfeits. They had too many real coins to bother with fakes. State officials hastened to reassure coin collectors that these companies were "very much above board, very honest and very legal" in selling their original coins. The only fair thing to do was to utilize the newspapers and the various trade journals to point out the difference between the counterfeits and the authentic coins so that these two companies would not be harmed when marketing their merchandise.

The accumulated evidence of the counterfeit coin fraud was turned over to the local Florida state attorney's office, but clamping down on the forgers and making the charges stick proved to be something else again. The counterfeiter could swear in court that he had never represented the coins as genuine, and the dealer could testify that he had been taken in, that he was also a victim. But whether the counterfeits were bought for trading or as an investment, they still represented possible disillusion and financial embarrassment to the dealer.

While these things went on ashore, the salvagers continued searching for more of the real treasure at sea. The Derelict routinely worked the Fort Pierce site and the Sebastian Inlet site alternately, depending on which had the clearer water. For a long time the salvagers suspected that since there was no ballast rock around the Cabin Wreck, then there must be another part of it nearby. But where?

They tried to figure out from which direction the hurricane had struck the fleet and where the ship had originally struck bottom. Fisher's crew came up with its magnetometer, a new model, and checked the area but found nothing. They broadened the search, using for the first time, at Clausen's insistence, a pattern. Then, nine hundred feet southwest of their original site, they found some cannon. Real Eight then moved the Derelict into the deeper water, and the divers went down. Within minutes they found three silver wedges. Treasure Salvors had discovered an unknown portion of the Cabin Wreck. These finds were soon followed by more. In the next several days, working with Treasure Salvors, Real Eight recovered several hundred loose pieces of eight, three clumps of corroded silver coins and ten 18-inch copper ingots weighing from thirty to seventy pounds each. But this was only the beginning. In the following week the record of their daily finds read like an inventory page from Fort Knox. Besides clumps and wedges, they brought up silver coins by the hundreds. One day's haul alone included 665 pounds of silver coins. At approximately fifteen coins to a pound, they had brought up almost 10,000 pieces of eight. A week later their total was almost a ton of silver coins!

Still the silver kept coming up. On July 7, ship's timbers were found; then, four days later, a 125-pound conglomerate of fused pieces of eight, sixty loose silver coins, two silver plates and an apothecary mortar were added to the haul.

So far the Cabin Wreck had produced something of everything—artifacts, china, gold, silver and jewelry. Finding and handling treasure daily destroyed the novelty of it. The salvagers doubted whether the wreck had anything else to offer them that would pique their treasure-jaded senses—but what turned up on July 24 proved them wrong.

Wagner's nephew, Rex Stocker, was examining a freshly blasted hole in the bottom when he saw something too startling to believe—a chest of silver. Without touching it, he rocketed to the surface and yelled out the good news to the divers on the Derelict.

Instead of reacting the way he thought they would, the men grinned and told him to go back to work. Everyone knew that treasure chests existed only in fiction. In tropical waters the hungry ship worms would have made quick work of any wooden containers that had fallen into the sea centuries ago.

But Stocker insisted. Finally Del Long consented to go down and look. Seconds later he shot to the surface, shouting that there was a treasure chest down there!

No divers ever grabbed their gear and tumbled over the side faster than the crew of the Derelict as they followed Long and Stocker back to the bottom.

Half buried in the sand was a blackish-brown wooden packing box just under two feet long, eleven inches wide and nine inches deep. Part of the top, one side and an end were missing, but the original contents were still there — three large clumps of silver coins solidly corroded together. The problem was how to get the 250-pound prize up intact without damaging it.

The divers worked for hours, finishing the work the blaster had begun, digging the chest out of the sand that had protected it from the wood-boring worms for 250 years. A large piece of plywood was brought down from the Derelict and slid under the chest; then, with part of the crew hauling on a line from above while the divers guided the plywood platform, the chest was hauled to the surface.

Once the extraordinary find was aboard the boat, the state salvage and exploration agent made sure that it was immersed in water to prevent the wood from drying out and warping before it could be preserved. The salvagers could only guess how many coins the chest contained, but their estimate of 3,000 was close.

The state's documentary research revealed that the chest contained 3,000 Troy ounces of silver in three 1,000-ounce bags. The 250 pounds was in four- and eight- real coins. At fifteen coins to a pound, there were about 3,750 of them in this conglomerate. At the preservation and research station in Tallahassee, the wood was examined and found to be Central American cedar. Precise measurements and a plan of the box were made to show its construction. Before the coins were cleaned and cataloged, a peculiar print of the corrosion products was noticed on one of the clumps. It was an impression of the fabric of the bag that had once held the coins. Clausen made a rubber cast of it, which provided the details for a drawing showing the fabric's intricate weave.

Word of the new find was quickly picked up by the news services. In the glare of publicity that followed, one seemingly insignificant fact was overlooked: besides the chest, the salvagers had found 1,500 loose silver coins that day.

With the August 1 recovery of 4,000 more pieces of eight and the early September visit of hurricane Betsy, the treasure hunters called a halt to the 1965 diving season—one that had netted them more than all the previous years combined. The total find for 1965 was 1,958 pounds 10 ounces of silver coins, or more than 37,000 of them; the 250-pound packing chest of silver coins in clumps; 1,782 gold coins; 41 disks of copper weighing thirty to seventy pounds each; 29 silver wedges; 12 silver "cupcakes" (ingots, so named because of their shape); an assortment of rings, earrings, brooches and miscellaneous jewelry; pieces of K'ang Hsi china, and thousands of historical artifacts, including ships' hardware, fastenings, and armament. Almost all the gold came from the Colored Beach Wreck, designated by the state as site 8-UW-l near Fort Pierce, and all but a fraction of the silver came from the Cabin Wreck south of Sebastian Inlet, classified as site 8-UW-2.

For the treasure salvagers no other year would ever be quite as rewarding as 1965 in terms of valuables found. From then on it was a downhill slide for Real Eight and Treasure Salvors . Other 1715 wrecks were found and worked, but the treasure hunters' fortunes rapidly waned. In 1966, for example, only 181 gold coins and 123 pounds 14.5 ounces of silver coins were found. However, a variety of artifacts, including several gold rings, silver wedges and cupcakes were also recovered. In 1967 the total of gold coins fell to 165; artifacts included 2 silver court sword hilts, silver sleeve links, silver crosses, segments of gold chain, 17 gold rings, several silver wedges, cupcakes and small clumps of silver coins. In 1968 the total fell to a low of 62 gold coins, 167 pounds of silver coins, some silverware and miscellaneous small silver and gold items. In 1969 the salvagers shifted their efforts to the Rio Mar Wreck near Vero Beach, possibly the remains of General Echeverz's Capitana, and had perhaps what was their second-best year. Although they found only 149 gold coins and 40 pounds 4 ounces of silver coins, they discovered numerous gold bars and valuable jewelry, including gold crosses and crucifixes. (See Appendix D for complete 1969 finds.) In 1970 the salvagers hit a new low, a total of 50 gold coins, 140 pounds of silver coins and approximately the same number of artifacts as in former years. With operational expenses running to hundreds of dollars a day, this kind of treasure hunting was fast becoming a losing proposition. The handwriting was on the wall.

This 400 year old ceramic jar survived intact.

Burgess explores a 1715 wreck site.

Author over a cannon muzzle.

Archaeologists documenting remains of the *San José*.

Artifacts cleaned and ready for display.

400 year old Chinese pottery that survived intact.

Many passengers' personal rings were found.

This long four-sided gold chain's links feature dog-flower blooms.

This solid gold dragon on an 11.5-foot gold chain is a whistle, toothpick and ear spoon certainly of Chinese origin.

Small gold tray is decorated with a flower motif.

This precious religious metal was purchased by the State for
$12,500 in coins.

A small treasure display is part of the Florida Museum in
Tallahassee's History and Archives building.

Chapter 15

Something More Valuable than Gold

Florida was involved in a hotly disputed double-handed game. On one hand she was licensing treasure hunters to lay waste historically valuable shipwrecks while they searched for coin, and on the other hand, she created the Bureau of Historic Sites and Properties and charged it with the responsibility of salvaging whatever archaeological information could be gleaned from the same sites. The two endeavors were incompatible with each other, but to a certain degree they worked. With but few refinements, mostly in the training of the state's field agents, the procedure was the same as that in use today: 90 percent of the digging by the treasure hunters is done with a blaster blowing a hole in the bottom sediments directly under the boat. Divers bring up all the artifacts and treasure found in the hole when the sand is blown away; then they move the boat to another place, blow the sand clear and again pick up what appears.

Each time artifacts come up from a hole dug by the salvagers, the state's technician, called a Salvage and Exploration Field Agent, takes a position reading with a sextant-like instrument from the stern of the boat on three surveyed landmarks. Later, when the site is being analyzed, the angles he has recorded are plotted on a chart.

The location of the hole that produced the artifacts is

found by triangulation. The technician attaches to every artifact recovered a plastic tag with a field inventory number, records where it came from, and sees that the day's archaeological finds are properly handled and stored for later transfer to the Bureau's Archaeological Research and Preservation Laboratory in Tallahassee.

Truckloads of artifacts eventually arrive at Tallahassee's History and Archives Building — the former county jail a few blocks from the capitol — where they are unloaded with the tender care usually associated with handling cases of eggs.

The artifacts are kept in the cellar of the old building, which has been converted into a $70,000 laboratory. In one of the many old jail cells behind thick steel and iron-barred doors, gold and silver coins are cleaned and cataloged. More perishable items are stored underwater in tubs, barrels and vats to await proper preservation and cataloging — a lengthy process which has resulted in a backlog of some 40,000 unprocessed artifacts.

In an effort to keep the salvage program manageable, the state issues salvage leases to only a relatively few firms that show they are qualified to carry out their contractual obligations. All applicants are closely screened. In addition they must put up $5,000 and $15,000 performance bonds with the state and pay $600 for a search contract and $1,200 for an actual salvage contract. A state man then goes along to supervise the salvage work.

When the full procedure of plotting the initial recovery of each artifact is continued on a wreck site over a period of several years, it results in hundreds of location points, which are then plotted on a master chart for the site at the Bureau. This gives the archaeologist an overall picture of the scattered finds and the scope of the wreck under investigation. From it he will learn exactly where the vessel struck and how it began breaking up, which is important in interpreting the disaster historically. The proximity of the artifacts and their relationship to one another suggest possible close relationships aboard the vessel before it wrecked. These are the clues that the archaeologist must have in order to reconstruct the event and learn something about the past, which may not yet be known.

Admittedly, this system is rudimentary when compared to the accuracy of land digs by trained archaeologists, or the accuracy obtained by underwater archaeologist Dr. George Bass in some of the University of Pennsylvania's expeditions to the Aegean, but it is as close as the state can get to the real thing under its present program of trying to combine science with commercial salvage.

The simple fact is that a very large chunk of our American heritage is being destroyed while licensed treasure hunters search for coins. And the irony of it all is that treasure hunting is a losing proposition, even for a concern that is working a relatively rich site. Long before the end, Real Eight Company readily admitted that it was spending $10,000 to $15,000 a month to bring up treasure worth in a good month maybe $10,000 to $14,000. As a result, in 1973 the company went bankrupt. What it amounts to is that both the salvagers and the public lose.

The Bureau's hope is that eventually three wreck-containing areas will be set aside by the state. In these areas the wrecks would not be worked for commercial purposes, but would be preserved for scientific research. This is not to suggest that the state go into the salvage business, only that these wrecks be sealed off until trained archaeologists can recover the historical information available from them. Florida waters contain from 1,800 to 2,000 shipwrecks, up to and past the World War II period. Possibly two hundred of these are of archaeological value to us, and a much smaller number have treasure potential. Unless these wrecks are protected, they will be destroyed. And there are no more where they came from.

Despite a growing public awareness of the need to preserve our ecological heritage, few people today are aware that they are losing an important piece of their historical heritage—that which can be found only in period shipwrecks. Public response to this statement might well be, "Who cares? What possible importance or significance is there in sifting through the bones of a ship that sank ages ago?"

An archaeologist or historian might explain by saying that period shipwreck sites constitute an extremely valuable source of information on the periods of exploration, colonization, trade and nationalization of hitherto undeveloped areas of the world. A ship, they might point out, was a single cultural entity; in effect, a "time capsule." It contained everything needed for living in one small area, things that were taken away from man in a moment in time. When these remains are found intact and their significance interpreted, scientists can literally reconstruct the past.

Such answers might be acceptable to academicians, but the lay public can generally understand better if it is given specific exam- pies. The presence of K'ang Hsi porcelain on the 1715 shipwrecks is sufficient to start a chain reaction of dramatic mental pictures when one learns that these pieces afford evidence of a unique trade route beginning in the Orient on the opposite side of the world from where they were found. From them one learns of the fabulous Manila galleon carrying the wealth of the Orient from the Philippine Islands across the Pacific in the longest continuous navigation in the world—a six-month voyage to Acapulco, Mexico. There, the merchandise was sold at a trade fair, the wares destined for Spain packed onto a mule train and carried across the mountains to the Gulf port of Vera Cruz for loading aboard the ships of the Flota. From there it went to Havana and then up the Florida Straits to the fleet's destruction by hurricane. Two hundred and fifty years later the delicate porcelain pieces—many still intact in their original packing clay—are found, mute evidence traceable to a Spanish trade route so rich that nations sent squadrons of ships halfway around the world to intercept and capture a Manila galleon. And in the 250-year history of that incredible trade route, they succeeded only four times. Such is the kind of story told by a piece of porcelain.

And there are others, less dramatic, perhaps, but equally important. Certain ceramic types, for example, whose age could be determined within a few years, were found on the wrecks, indicating that Spanish travelers had taken heirlooms with them dating from one hundred years before the storm and the wrecks. Or the surprising discovery of four-tined forks on the 1715 wrecks, when it had been believed that the Spanish used nothing but three-tined forks. That fourth tine bridged an important historical gap. Archaeologists now knew that during the late 17th and early 18th centuries the English were eating with three-tined forks while the Spanish and French were eating with four. The different styles of fork used in these countries reflected custom and usage. The fact that the use of four-tined forks spread from France to Spain and then to England probably indicates the transmittal of other ideas. During the late 17th and early 18th centuries, the concepts of individual rights and laws which are now a part of our western civilization arose in France with the period of Enlightenment, spread to Spain through the political influence of France on that country, and subsequently to England, from which they came to our country. Such small clues as the tine of a fork are often highly significant pieces in a much larger historical puzzle.

Understandably, then, archaeologists are somewhat more than annoyed at the idea of treasure or curio hunters vacuum-cleaning a historically valuable shipwreck for coins, when scientists need every available fragment of evidence left as it was found, in relationship to the whole, if they ever hope to learn anything significant from the find. What archaeologists try to recover from a shipwreck is far more valuable than treasure. Their methods take longer and are considerably more meticulous. Much of what is recovered consists of everyday items that relate to a past historical period, and this is where we are very short. One of the questions most often asked of underwater archaeologists is, "Why do you need these things off shipwrecks when the museums are filled with them?" Unfortunately, our museums are not filled with these kinds of things. The objects that survive in museums and private collections are only the best examples of a culture: the best weapons, the best silverware, the best paintings. These fail to represent a whole culture. To get as accurate a picture as possible, archaeologists have to dig it all, the outhouses as well as the temples. Yet, they are still dealing only with a statistical sample, which is what archaeology is concerned with today. With a shipwreck they are dealing only with the hard parts that survive. And this is usually so limited that every piece counts if the archaeologist is to do a creditable job of bringing forth that culture.

Here is how such an operation would be carried out by a team of archaeologists. Suppose they are looking for a particular wreck to fill out a gap in their records. For example, assume that they have worked an English ship, which sank in 1750 and another which sank in 1725 or 1730. To fill a gap in their information and refine their data, they might profitably look for a 1740 English wreck.

The first tip on the general location of such a wreck might come from archival records. An exhaustive search of English sources may be made — in the Public Records Office, admiralty records, Lloyds, the British Museum. Once a likely suspect is found that was lost in Florida waters, all that ship's records are acquired. Usually with the English, court-martial records are extremely useful, so these documents are carefully analyzed, checked and rechecked. From this work will usually emerge several areas, possibly reefs, where the ship might have gone down. Sometimes it is as easy as the name of the reef itself. Looe Key, Triumph Reef, Ledbetter Reef, Carysfort Reef are all areas named for lost ships. Other times it is more difficult. There may be several prime areas in which to look for the wreck.

A search of a suspect area is made by a boat towing a

magnetometer. When the instrument detects and records a magnetic anomaly on the bottom, the spot is marked with a buoy, and divers go down to see what they have. It may be nothing more than a cast iron sewer pipe; nine times out of ten it will be a modern wreck. But the tenth time the divers may find what they are looking for—an old wreck, overlaid perhaps by ballast rock.

Next, a test excavation is made and a sample of artifacts taken for examination. Ceramic sherds or other evidence often tells the archaeologist something about the period and nationality of the vessel. Along with other artifacts, ballast stones might be recovered for petrological analysis. Since early sailing vessels tended to carry a particular kind of ballast stone—the size, shape and type varied considerably according to origin—identification and analysis may provide more vital clues to the nationality of the ship.

If the wreck appears to be the one the archaeologists are searching for, another magnetic survey is run on a smaller scale to plot more accurately the ferrous components of the wreck. This is usually done by a boat pulling the sensing element of the magnetometer systematically over the site, using a north-south, east-west grid pattern. Or, conditions permitting, the same grid pattern can be swum by a diver carrying the magnetometer head and working along a compass-oriented single line, which can be moved to ten-foot parallel intervals at the end of each run. Anomalies are recorded on the instrument's moving graph tape on the surface. When the entire area has been checked by the magnetometer, all of the anomalies are then plotted on a chart so that the archaeologist has an accurate record of the ferrous components of the wreck and their relationship to one another. They show the wreck's distribution and the main concentrations or epicenters of iron where the large excavation might begin.

If ballast rocks and wreckage are visible on the ocean floor, an underwater photogrammetric survey of the site follows. This is made in stereo with a six-foot-long winglike metal structure on which two cameras are mounted parallel to each other at opposite ends of the device. As this "wing" is swum through the water on a compass-oriented course at a precise elevation over the site, the two cameras take simultaneous overlapping photographs of everything on the bottom. Later, one set of pictures, fitted together in a mosaic, gives the archaeologist a composite photo-map of the site, while the other is consulted to compute the elevations of any objects extending above the level of the sea floor. Additional photogrammetric photos will be made of features or details of the vessel as they are revealed by the excavation. From these a highly accurate picture of the site emerges. At this point, a sub-bottom profiler may be used to penetrate the sediment over or around the wreck. This device, using low-frequency sound waves, can give the archaeologist helpful information by recording the densities of the sediments in the area.

Using all the information gathered, the archaeologist selects a place on the site where he reasons he can make his most productive excavation, getting the maximum number of artifacts. Before beginning, however, it is necessary for him to find nearby a relatively "clean" area free of artifacts, where ballast stones from the wreck can be placed as they are recorded and removed from the pile. Usually, this will be a wide sandy spot to which all the unwanted remains of the wreck will be eventually shifted when the original site has been completely excavated. Sometimes these areas are covered with three to five feet of sand, which the archaeologist excavates with the blower until bedrock is reached. All artifacts found there are photographed, tagged and removed.

At this stage the archaeologist has a record of what can be "seen" magnetically and a record of what can be seen photographically, and he begins to take off the top layer of ballast rock to learn what lies beneath. As divers remove the stones, they may find artifacts. These are tagged and their

220

location recorded, generally through a photographic grid sometimes set up over the area on a scaffold. This may be a one-and-a-half- or two-meter square aluminum or angle-iron frame enclosing a decimeter square grid. The horizontal and vertical lines of the wire grid serve as a control for photographs or drawings made from above to show the relationship of all visible items within the frame before they are picked up.

Next, the blower aboard the research boat slowly fans sand away from the test site. As artifacts appear, the archaeologist continues to photograph, tag and remove them. Once all the ballast stones have been removed, the divers reach the bottom of the ship, where they may find broken cannon and anchors sometimes carried by vessels as additional ballast. These are photographed in place and removed. Next to be recorded are any timbers and frames remaining from the structure of the ship. These are particularly important, for few details are known about marine architecture prior to 1650.

Most of the productive work on the main part of the site has now been done. There may be other wreckage under the sand along the sides of the wreck, and there is usually a large amount of material fanned out by tides, currents and storms to one quadrant of the main wreck. Although the archaeologist may not want to pick up everything in the fanned scattering, he may wish to place test excavations there. It is therefore possible for him to go from a continuous excavation on the main body of the wreck to a discontinuous one in other areas of the site.

As he works along the edge of the wreck, he will probably uncover remnants of the standing rigging. Areas beyond this may provide parts of the vessel's superstructure. Each new excavation proceeds as with the ballast stones — a gradual layer-by-layer analysis which continues until bedrock is reached or until there is no longer any wreckage to be found.

All recovered artifacts are immersed in containers of salt

water aboard the boat and later transported to the laboratory, where they are cleaned, analyzed and restored. After this may come more archival research. If the vessel is one that is known about but not yet identified, the archaeologist may learn the significance of the find and be able to contribute new information from the evidence. All the archaeological and historical data are then written into a wreck report documenting the site.

It is easy to see that this operation is totally incompatible with treasure hunting. However, something must be said for the accomplishments of a state-operated program in which treasure and archaeological artifacts are being recovered simultaneously. Despite its problems and shortcomings, such a program has resulted in Florida's now owning some 50,000 artifacts relating to 17th-, 18th-, and 19th-century shipwrecks worked by treasure-salvage firms under contract to the state. In the nine years this program has been in effect, this policy of paying salvagers for their efforts in recovering underwater treasure has resulted in the state's owning what will one day, with proper exchanges and management, be the best collection of Spanish colonial coins in the world, primarily because to date the state has kept intact the 25 percent it retains. In other words, Florida citizens can claim as their public property such unique objects as a large medallion bearing a likeness of a woman and a dog, valued at $17,000, and some 1,100 (as of 1969) gold coins, including some extremely rare issues, among which are several Phillip V 8-escudo pieces known to be worth from $10,000 to $15,000. In addition, there is nearly a ton of silver coins which have yet to be analyzed and an assortment of jewelry such as earrings, crosses and rings. The entire collection is valued at an estimated $1,000,000. (At the time it was recovered.)

No value has yet been set on the historical artifacts, nor is one likely to be. The eventual destinations of all the finds are museums, particularly those of Florida's Division of Recreation and Parks. At present, some of the material is on permanent exhibit at the McLarty State Museum, at Sebastian State Park on the Florida east coast near the site of the old Spanish survivors' and salvagers' camp, and at Pepper Park State Museum, St. Lucie State Park, Fort Pierce. Two other museums now in the planning stage will also have permanent exhibits — one in Key West and another in conjunction with a new History and Archives Building scheduled for completion at Tallahassee in 1976. Three commercial enterprises also house treasure and artifacts recovered by salvagers: The Real Eight Museum of Sunken Treasure at Cape Canaveral, Art McKee's Treasure Fortress at Plantation Key, and Treasure Salvors' exhibit of treasure aboard the Golden Doubloon, a 500-ton, 160-foot replica of a Spanish galleon at Key West.

The material presented at the state facilities has been arranged in line with modern museum methods. Instead of being thrown in with a great many similar objects like random gold coins, which are about as impressive to look at as a plaqueful of arrowheads, a few coins may be displayed on a map of the world, for example, showing the products produced by various countries in the year 1715. The museum-goer may be astonished to learn from this display that there was a university at Cuzco, Peru, almost a century before there was one in North America, or that there was a mint in Mexico City striking coins almost 250 years before there was a United States. Instead of just "things" to look at, here will be something to be remembered. Instead of remaining stray items of unrelated interest, the treasure and artifacts will be used to give people an overall picture of history. They will leave this kind of interpretive museum with a better understanding of early-18th-century shipbuilding, trade routes, minting methods and the products of certain sections of the world in early times.

And perhaps, after all the studies are made and all the facts are in, this wealth of historical information from early shipwreck sites will prove to be the most valuable treasure of all.

ABOUT THE AUTHORS

As a freelance writer/photographer Robert F. Burgess writes non-fiction articles and books about his favorite subjects—underwater exploration, treasure hunting, sharks, shipwrecks, sailing, and sea mysteries. Describing his various experiences in the underwater world his articles and books are written in a manner that put readers into the events they are reading about. Whether uncovering a long lost Spanish galleon, exploring an underwater cave, losing a camera in a prehistoric forest, fighting a 12 foot tiger shark, or photographing scientists recovering the remains of Ice Age Man from sunken caverns, you will be there. Like reading fiction, Bob's style makes it easy for readers to experience the excitement of these events without their dangers. His pursuit of unusual adventures has taken him through Europe into North Africa and into the tropical Caribbean Sea. Pick a title from his books and feel free to join him anywhere along the way!

Carl J. Clausen is a marine archaeologist whose principal interests lay in colonial-period shipwreck sites. He has served as Adjunct Professor of North American Archaeology at the American Institute of Nautical Archaeology, as well as a university lecturer and a consultant to private firms. Mr. Clausen supervised Florida's treasure salvage program and later assisted Texas in similar archaeological shipwreck investigations at Padre Island. He headed up a major archaeological exploration of Ice Age Man's habitation sites found in deep Florida Springs that date back to 12,000 Years Before Present Time as described in Burgess' books *The Cave Divers,* and *Man, 12,000 Years Under the Sea.*

Both authors live in northwest Florida.

3-CHARTS-IN-ONE SNORKELERS' AND DIVERS' GUIDE TO OLD SHIPWRECKS OF FLORIDA'S SOUTHEAST COAST

This publication graphically details locations of old shipwrecks lost off Florida's southeast coast including those of the Spanish Treasure Fleets of 1715 and 1733. Three true compass ranges are furnished for each wreck along with a thumbnail history providing name of the vessel, water depth, when lost, its cargo, and what salvors found. Computerized scatter patterns of found treasure extend for a mile along beaches opposite some wrecks. Coin-hunters still find treasure there today! Printed on both sides of heavy bond buff-colored paper, the 20 x 28-inch chart is folded to 7 x 9-inches and comes in a waterproof envelope.. To learn more go on-line and enter
http://www.fairpoint.net/~hunterb4/oldwrck.html

To order, use PayPal or send check or Money Order for $25.95 to

Robert Burgess
308 West Marion St.
Chattahoochee, FL 32324

Appendix A

ORDER FROM THE KING Initiating The Flota Portion Of The 1715 Fleet "Proyecto of the Crown to the Council of the Indies: 3 March 1712." Printed 28 June 1712, Madrid. Nine pages, translated.

Since the continued navigation to the Indies is the main and most important essential for the good of the Monarchy, its vassals and its commerce, which produces not only the major source of financial help in times of urgency, but the opulent trade of its vassals, who share in its so widespread fruits; and since there follows from the greater security and improvement of the dominions of the Indies and the avoidance of illegal commerce in them …His Majesty wishes and orders that, this present year of 1712, there be made ready and sail for the Kingdom of New Spain a flotilla consisting of eight vessels, among which shall be numbered a Capitana, an Almiranta, first and second pataches, and the four listed merchant ships, in the following form:

I. That, for Capitana and Almiranta of the said fleet, it remains for His Majesty to stipulate the form of those two vessels and their contract, as well as for the persons who must go under orders in them. His Majesty must decide on these points with the greatest dispatch so that these matters might be publicly known.

II. That, with regard to the first patache. His Majesty will also advise about it; as to the second patache, the Tribunal of the Casa de Contratacion, using their privilege, may name it and make their selection known. Its owner, however, must be a Spaniard. The choice of a particular vessel to fill this place must, moreover, be made known within thirty days after the publication of this order. It may be up to 200 or even 250 tons capacity. After having given notice of its selection, the Tribunal must furnish precise information about the vessel to the Council of the Indies, which will then inform His Majesty. If the thirty-day term passes without the Tribunal having made any announcement, His Majesty may make the choice, with all the promptness needed to insure the fleet's departure on time. If it appears to the Council that it is His Majesty's will that the first patache should not exceed the second in size, the data shall be present for His Majesty's study, when he shall choose to name the vessel.

III.   That, for the four merchant ships, which as might be supposed are included in the total of eight vessels, they are hereinafter named by His Majesty. The first shall be that vessel of the 300 tons lading license — a privilege enjoyed by special grant by the Seminary of the City of Seville. This choice must be made within thirty days, under the same above-mentioned requirements for the second patache to be chosen by the Tribunal.

The second, named Nuestra Señora de Regia, San Francisco Xavier y San Joseph, has as owner D. Pedro Bernardo Peralta y Cordoba and is now found opposite the Barranco of the Cadiz interest, having failed to find a place in the last fleet which sailed for New Spain.

The third, named Nuestra Señora del Rosario, San Francisco Xavier y las Animas, has as its owner D. Francisco de Chaves Espinosa de los Monteros, and is found at the same place for the same reason.

For the fourth vessel, it shall be that for which His Majesty lately granted concession in the Council consulta of 22 December 1711 to D. Juan de Castro y Aldao. His vessel shall not exceed 400 tons, notwithstanding the fact that His Majesty had previously conceded him the right in the consulta of a ship of up to 600 tons. It is now seen that the ship in the said fleet should be of the more moderate size, in order to facilitate its more rapid departure and quick return. It is thus ordered that this ship must expressly make its appearance in the Bay of Cadiz within thirty days of the publication of this order in Seville. If it does not, then the grant shall be rendered null and void for this occasion, although it may be used at a future date. In that event, the billet for this vessel shall remain, in order that the two-thirds lading privilege pertaining to Seville might be fulfilled; the merchants of Seville shall make their ship selection known within eight days following the thirty days. Failing this, then neither party shall any longer possess the right; then His Majesty will choose.

The reason His Majesty has not listed ships corresponding to the two-thirds lading permission of Seville on this occasion is due to the fact that the University of Navigators had advised that they had no ship opposite their Tribunal. For that reason, the grant which pertains to them does not apply. In order that this right should be credited to them for future fleets, it should be well understood that with regard to the billet-space of the wine growers of that city, it should be verified in accordance with their rule and practice. With regard, then, to the 300 tons of the Seminary, they can load in that ship as well as in that of D. Castro y Aldao and in the first and second pataches the fruits of the growers in accordance with the rules which ordinarily apply. This leaves for the growers of Cadiz the two ships of Don Pedro de Cordoba and D. Francisco de Chaves, which pertain to that Tribunal.

IV.   That, if His Majesty be advised that a ship named Santo Cristo de San Roman owner: D. Juan Antonio de Equilaz, which served as Almiranta in the fleet under the command of D. Diego de Santillan, His Majesty wishes this vessel to go as Capitana or Almiranta of this fleet. If the matter is negotiated, and the said D. Juan agrees with His Majesty under the rules and in the form with which a commander whom he wished to go could be named, for this purpose agreement might be reached, in virtue of the power he has before His Majesty to treat of it. If he fails, or excuses himself from performance, His Majesty will have to avail himself of the ship for that purpose under the rules and in the form always practiced for this purpose in similar cases.

If this should happen, His Majesty will then name the person who will go as commander, under the form and circumstances which His Majesty will then declare. His Majesty orders the Council to bring to the Royal notice that which results from the summons made to the said Don Juan Antonio de Equilaz.

V.   That the said fleet must go out to sail from the Bay of Cadiz by the last day of July of this year, without any delay. To this end, His Majesty declares that any of the four merchant ships or the two pataches which are not promptly ready to receive cargo from the tenth to the fifteenth of June will be excluded from the voyage. For this purpose, His Majesty orders that legal notice of this be given to the shipowners, so that none might plead ignorance of it, and so that it might be known that the fleet will sail without fail on the appointed day with those ships which are ready.

VI.   That the body of merchants ought to, and can, carry for trade in the said ships, and in those to be named as Capitana and Almiranta, all the goods and products which they wish. Before departure they shall pay the same fees and duties fixed and paid in the ships which sailed for New Spain under the command of D. Andres de Arriola. This shall be done under the same rules, formalities and provisions contained in the proyecto agreed upon and fixed for that outfitting, without any departures whatsoever from the proyecto, which must be scrupulously observed.

VII.   That the same rules and fixed duties may be observed on the return to Spain, without any difference whatsoever, and with equal force with regard to entry and departure from the Indies and to any penalties applicable, whether to this part or to the preceding sixth section.

VIII.   That His Majesty will name ministers in Cadiz and Seville to collect the duties of departure and return. The sending of customs-house permits, the readying of ships, and the registers shall be in their charge—all this in conformity with that which was expressed in the last fleet's proyecto. The council shall send to each the same instructions, together with copies of the proyectos cited, so that they might understand what took place in the dispatch of the last fleet under D. Andres de Arriola.

IX.   That, with regard to the freight rates which merchants must pay to ship-owners for goods, effects and products loaded for the outward, or homeward, journey—these shall be precisely the same prices which were fixed in the proyecto of D. Andres de Arriola's fleet. Thus, questions and embarrassments among merchants and ship-owners can be avoided.

X.   His Majesty declares that, in the two ships serving as Capitana and Almiranta, there shall be loaded on the account of the Royal Exchequer 2,000 quintales of mercury, a publication of bulls, and two years' supply of stamped paper for New Spain. All of this shall be divided so that half of it shall go in each ship. These things shall be taken to Vera Cruz to be delivered to the persons or Ministers destined to receive them. To this end, all of the customary obligations shall be made.

XI.   Also, that the first and second patches shall carry for the account of the Royal Exchequer and without cost to it, one thousand quintales of mercury—500 in each, and under the same regulations found in the tenth section above.

XII. That the said merchant ships and patches shall pay the Seminary its usual alms-payment, as in other voyages, without altering it, or providing less than in the past.

XIII. That, if the Capitana of the Windward Fleet, which has most lately been under the command of D. Andres de Arriola, arrives in Spain before the date fixed for the departure of this fleet—it is His Majesty's will that this ship with all its equipment and the major and minor officials which sail in her shall be placed in careenage. She shall then be readied, supplied and armed for the account of the Royal Exchequer in the form and under the rules which His Majesty shall prescribe. Then she shall sail back with the two ships named in this fleet. They shall sail under her command and flag as Capitana. If His Majesty has already chosen the ships to serve as Capitana and Almiranta, then the one selected as Capitana shall become Almiranta, and that chosen Almiranta shall become reserve Almiranta. This shall be done in such order that there shall follow no prejudice to those already chosen, nor to the Capitana of the Windward Fleet during its stay here. Thus will be avoided the great expense and harm which would result to the Royal Exchequer, and also the gap which this vessel would leave if it were long missing from the Windward Fleet. It is also the Royal will of His Majesty that, if the said Capitana comes in time to return to the Indies with the fleet as its Capitana, His Majesty declares that it must carry for the Royal account 3,000 quintales of mercury and the duplicate of the publication of bulls which the other two ships must carry, and also the supplies of rigging, fittings, canvas and iron and other things needed for the ships of the Windward Fleet. It shall also carry other items which His Majesty must resolve should be made in those Kingdoms. And if it should appear that this should exceed the load advisable for the said Capitana of Barlovento, His Majesty will order that it be loaded with those things with which it should be concerned.

XIV.   That if His Majesty should resolve that the said Capitana of the Windward Fleet shall not return to Spain with the said fleet, the ship which had been serving as Almiranta shall again become Capitana; the reserve Almiranta shall become Almiranta, etc.

XV. With regard to the return of the said fleet, it shall remain for His Majesty to send confidential orders when needed and also to advise the riches which they are to bring for the Royal Exchequer, and how much shall be carried in each vessel. The Council shall issue whatever orders might seem appropriate with regard to their fees and other fiscal measures.

XVI. That it is also left to His Majesty to name those persons who shall go as disputados [commercial representatives] of the said fleet, under the same regulations and in the same form in which His Majesty named them for the last fleet of D. Andres de Arriola.

XVII. That, for the execution of and obedience to all that which has been expressed here. His Majesty orders that the Council send copies of these orders to the Casa de Contratacion, the Consulado of Seville, and the same in Cadiz, Puerto de Santa Maria and San Lucar and to the second who shall make it known in the Junta General de Comercio. Thus knowing these exact orders, the members of these bodies shall be enabled to make their plans for employment and shiploading of their goods and fruits.

XVIII. And that also the Tribunal is ordered to notify the owners of the ships named in these orders that they should soon be in Cadiz. Thus within eight days of the receipt of this order they might put their ships into careenage. The owners of other ships yet to be chosen should be advised to do the same. The Tribunal should advise the Council by each mail of the exact status of preparations and the Council shall inform His Majesty. Now His Majesty orders that for no reason nor for any case whatsoever shall any request for admittance to the fleet be considered; His Majesty declares that he shall not augment it, because this best suits His Royal service and the most prompt success of this most important affair. It would only be possible for other ships to go if they go in company with others or if they take registry for ports other than Vera Cruz and do not enter it surreptitiously. Madrid, 3 March 1712. Don Joseph de Grimaldo.

(This is a copy of the original proyecto which His Majesty remitted to the Council of the Indies for their obedience and execution. Madrid, 28 March 1712.)

Appendix B

THE FLEETS' MANIFESTS IN THE NEW WORLD

CT 2400

Galeones

Loaded at Cartagena, July and August 1714. Ladings certified before the Governor and Royal Officials.

1. Capitana (partial lading)
47 leather bags of cacao, equal to 310 arrobas, 16 lb.
300 quintales of brazilwood
4,695 pesos 6 reales, in three gold bars and in doubloons
3,002 pesos 2 reales, in two gold bars
1,530 pesos 1 1/2 reales, in one gold bar
2,139 pesos 5 reales, in one gold bar and doubloons
18 marks 5 1/2 oz. of silver
175 pesos 8 reales in plata doble
5,283 pesos 1 1/2 reales in four bars and doubloons
2,000 pesos: 1,000 in doubloons and 1,000 in plata doble
400 pesos in doubloons
1,150 pesos in doubloons
100 pesos in doubloons
210 pesos in doubloons
A gold chain with 50 pesos and 4 tomines; ley 20 carats @ 20 reales, worth 126 pesos, 2 reales.
Another gold chain with 85 pesos and 1 tomin; ley 21 1/2 carats [21 1/2 reales, worth 228 pesos, 6 reales].
A small gold chain of 10 Castellanos weight, 3 tomines [@17

reales, equals 26 pesos, 6 reales].

2. Nao Nuestra Señora de la Concepcion — Master, Don Diego Pablo Soliac. Her register is set up in Cartagena from 17 July 1714 to 20 August 1714.
740 half-hides, in pelt 105 quintales of brazilwood 100 quintales of brazilwood
8 leather sacks of cacao
2 leather sacks of cacao
1 chest of vanilla
80 quintales of brazilwood 700 tanned hides 80 quintales of brazilwood
3 leather sacks of cacao
4,714 pesos 3 reales; 1 gold bar and doubloons
3,000 pesos in doubloons
25 bales of paper of 32 reams each 6 chests of nails
3 boxes of locks
1 bale of dry goods
She is to be further loaded in Havana with other goods.

3. Fregata — **Navio Nuestra Señora del Rosario** (Almiranta) — Master, Don Manuel
Albarez. Lading at Cartagena, 20 July 1714.
50 quintales of brazilwood
20 leather sacks of cacao
1 cajon [chest]
650 half-hides; 325 whole ones
4 chests of chocolate
8 leather sacks of cacao
1 chest of gifts
2 chests of shells of Carey
2 little chests and 1 small jar for the Fiscal of the Council of the Indies
4,695 pesos 6 reales in 4 gold bars; the rest in doubloons
3,546 pesos 6 reales in 2 gold bars; the rest in doubloons
175 pesos in plata doble

5,283 pesos 1 1/2 reales; 4 gold bars and doubloons
2,000 pesos in doubloons
75 half-pieces of crudos [probably untanned leathers]
3 chests of dry goods
6 barrels of copperas.

The manifest also mentions the "fregata francesa, El Cierbo," which was taken on the Porto Bello coast: "this frigate, the said other sloop and frigate, the Fregata San Miguel, taken on the coast." Later, this vessel was loaded with 192 quintales of brazilwood.

Mexico 486B
Flota

Loaded at Vera Cruz, 4 May 1715. The officials of the Royal Hacienda of this city of the New Vera Cruz and the port of San Juan de Ulúa for His Majesty: Treasurer Francisco San Juan de Santacruz of the Tribunal of the Contaduria, member of the Royal Consejo de Hacienda Contador; Don Juan de Echagaray, Factor Veedor; Don Lorenzo de la Torre, Caballero of the Order of Calatrava — both named as Gentlemen by His Majesty — and the official Royal supernumerary, Pagador Don Juan Manuel de Santellises:

We certify that in the Capitana, Almiranta, resfuerzo and patache which comprise the fleet under the command of General Juan Esteban de Ubilla (which is ready to sail on the return voyage to the Kingdoms of Castile) there are loaded, registered and declared, for the account of His Majesty and of the different interested parties and individuals, the quantities of pesos, cochineal, indigo and other items which we will itemize as follows:

FOR THE ACCOUNT OF HIS MAJESTY

The following are divided equally between the Almiranta and the Capitana:

For the King in reales and bars: 209,279 pesos 6 reales 1 gr.
For the Chamber of the Queen our Lady, in doubloons and reales: 80,000 pesos
For Salaries of the Council of the Indies: 160,248 pesos 6 reales 1 gr.
For the Treasury of the Council, benefices: 8,800 pesos
For the Secretary of the Council, fines: 63 pesos
President of Guadalajara, reales: 4,279 pesos 3 reales
Product of Bulls of the Crusade; reales and bars: 124,279 peso 1 real 6 gr.
Alms for the Blessed Souls of the Monte de Piedad: 671 pesos 6 reales 6 gr.
Alms for the hospitals of Cadiz and the Royal Hospital in Galicia: 8,000 pesos
For the Duke of Tubenasso: 5,000 pesos
Of product of Royal mercury, remitted by D. Juan Joseph de Beitia; reales and bars: 518,469 pesos 3 reales
Product of the sales and composition of lands and waters, sent by D. Francisco de Balensuela: 24,000 pesos
For the Convent of the Merced Calcaza of Madrid, sent by the same: 15,831 pesos 4 reales
For Vacancies of Bishoprics: 6,319 pesos 3 reales
For Quarter-vacancies of same: 7,232 pesos 4 reales
Donation of the ecclesiastical Cabildo of la Puebla: 2,000 pesos
Donation of Haciendas: 350 pesos
Donation of the Sr. Archbishop of Mexico: 4,000 pesos
For the Royal Treasury of Havana: 44,000 pesos

(total) 1,222,834 pesos 3 tomines 5 gr.

FOR THE ACCOUNTS OF PRIVATE INDIVIDUALS

Capitana

In coins and bars in 8,086 small chests and sacks 2,559,917 pesos
730 leather bags of fine cochineal
241 leather bags and chests of indigo
23 chests of worked silver
6 chests of gifts
17 chests of vanillas [vanilla beans]
62 chests of chocolate
70 sheets of copper
730 tanned leathers
4 chests of Chinese porcelain
100 quintales of brazilwood
9 chests of earthenware vessels
1 small chest of dust [powder?] of Oaxaca
14 earthen jugs of balsam
1 small chest with small gold bars, doubloons and pearls

Almiranta

In silver and bars, in 684 small chests and sacks: 2,076,004 pesos
728 leather bags of cochineal
1,702 leather bags and chests of indigo
139 sheets of copper 682 tanned leathers
26 chests of earthenware vessels
48 chests of vanillas
85 chests of gifts
8 earthen jugs of balsam and liquid amber
2 chests with writing desks

40 chests of chocolate and dust of Oaxaca
2 chests of bath oil
30 leather sacks of wild cochineal
12 chests of annatto [a red dyestuff]
53 chests of worked silver 14 chests of Chinese porcelain
80 bales of lurga of Talapa
3 folding-screens [?] — biohos [sic]
9 leather sacks of cacao
500 quintales of brazilwood
31 bales of sarsaparilla

resfuerzo

Coined money (silver) in 81 small chests and loose leather
bags: 252,171 pesos
13 chests of worked silver
280 leather sacks of fine cochineal
595 leather sacks of indigo
3,320 tanned leathers
21 barrels and earthen jugs of liquid amber
257 half-hides with hair [pelts]
6 earthen jugs of balsam
198 bales of cathartic
75 chests of earthenware vessels
30 chests of chocolate
19 bales of cacao
22 chests of vanillas
500 quintales of brazilwood
11 bales of powdered hellebore root
136 chests of gifts
77 leather sacks and chests of wild cochineal
300 hides with hair [pelts]
3 biobos [sic] probably biombos [folding screens]
32 chests of Chinese porcelain
65.5 quintales of sarsa [sarsaparilla?]
2 bales of quinine

1 chest of sugar
2 sheets of copper
4 chests with writing desks
16 chests of copal [a brittle resin]
13 chests of annatto
7 quintales of sassafras

patache

In 12 chests and loose sacks: 44,000 pesos
63 leather bags of fine cochineal
169 leather bags and chests of indigo
870 tanned hides
8 alfardas [wood beams?]
200 quintales of brazilwood
9 barrels of liquid amber
25 leather sacks of wild cochineal
58 boxes [chests] of gifts
81 bales of cathartic
18 chests of chocolate
57 dichos of earthenware vessels
3 bales of powdered hellebore root
4 trunks
1 bale of quinine
7 chests of Chinese porcelain
8 bales of roots of Michoacan
7 chests of vanillas
11 bales of cacao
12 earthen jugs of oil of betto
1 chest of annatto 16 earthen jugs of copal

Inasmuch as the coined and bar silver, the doubloons and
gems and other types of merchandise whose details are
itemized above are those which have been loaded, registered
and declared in the said Capitana, Almiranta, resfuerzo and
patache (for the account of His Majesty and of private

persons) in accord with the details expressed in the registros and in order to advise His Majesty, we sign this instrument by virtue of the letter of order of the most Excellent Señor the Duke of Linares, Viceroy of New Spain, Governor and Captain-General also, under the date of 4 May 1715; for duplicate we now give this to you by virtue of the order of the Most Excellent Señor Marquis de Valer, Viceroy, Governor and Captain-General of this Kingdom. 4 June 1716. (There follows a summary of all cargoes in total, by type. The merchandise is not listed again; there is shown below the totals of bullion, coin, etc., in the four ships.)

The shipments of:
Real Hacienda (The King's Share) 1,222,824 pesos 3 tomines 5
    grains
Private Persons   4,932,092 pesos

Total   6,154,916 pesos 3 tomines 5
    grains

Appendix C

DETAILS AND ANALYSIS OF THE RECOVERED TREASURE

Specifically, the treasure included 6 circular-shaped silver ingots, the largest weighing 27 pounds, and 6 similar disks of gold, weighing from 1 pound 15 ounces to 8 pounds 5 ounces; a silver bar weighing 35 pounds 8 1/2 ounces; 11 free-form flat "puddles" of silver weighing together 5 pounds 4 ounces; 16 whole gold rings and the two halves of another; 8 pieces of gold chain bearing an intricate floral design, the longest length 2.04 meters; 3 buckles, two of silver and another of gold; 5 fragmentary silver forks and parts of several silver spoons and knife handles; 2 silver plates; a pair of ornate silver candlestick tops with threaded stems, as if they had been disassembled from their missing bases; several unidentified bullet-shaped objects; 200 pounds of silver coins and slightly more than 3,700 gold coins.

The prevalent form for the bulk precious metals was a circular-shaped ingot with a rounded bottom, evidently formed either by allowing the molten metal to cool in a crucible with a generally rounded bottom or by pouring the metal into a similarly shaped mold. The rough, porous bottoms of most of the ingots indicated that the mold may have been of stone. Markings were found on the top surfaces of the largest of the silver disks. The largest gold disks were stamped with Roman numerals, sometimes followed by from one to three small circles. For example, the gold disk weighing 8 pounds 5 ounces was stamped "XIII" followed by two circles arranged one above the other. Another, weighing 7 pounds 3 ounces, was marked "X" while a third, also weighing 7 pounds 3 ounces, was marked "XI" followed by three circles as well as a ragged assayer's bite where a sample had evidently been clipped from the ingot at the mint by the king's assayer to test the amount of gold in the piece. The smallest gold disk was stamped five times with three stamps. First was a large octagonal stamp near the center of the disk. Inside and slightly below the center of this stamp was a large "S" surmounted by a crown. To the left of the "S" was a small "m," above and below which were round unidentifiable figures, possibly rosettes. To the right was a small letter "o" with the same round figures above and below. These central symbols were enclosed in a border of two ridges, one inside the other, separated by a series of dots. A second stamp across the disk contained the Roman numerals "XXII," below a small crown. The disk was struck twice with this stamp, above and below the large central stamp just described. The third stamp, used both to the right and to the left, was a shield containing a crown above and an almost indiscernible figure below.

The crowns suggest that all of these are probably royal stamps. The "m" and "o" characters identify the piece as originating in, or having passed through, the Mexico City mint. F. Xavier Calico of Barcelona, president of the International Association of Professional Numismatists and an authority on Spanish colonial coins, believes that the large "S" in the center stamp may indicate that the piece dates from around 1700, when Jose Sarmiento was Viceroy of New Spain. Another authority reports that crown seals were used on ingots which had not yet passed through the royal foundry and upon which royal dues were still owed. The Roman numeral stamp "XXII" is believed to indicate the gold content of the disk in carats.

Spectrographic analysis indicated that the disks were an approximately half-gold, half-silver alloy. Since all of them received at least one assayer's bite, or bocado, the markings may show the purity of the gold in quilates or carats, with the small circles representing grains (four per carat). Considering the relatively low gold content of the disk, Clausen felt that the markings represented a stage in the refining of the metal.

The largest disk was marked "1659" or "1699," "01230," and

"MI" in three rows on its pitted upper surface. The disk appeared to be gold, but analysis showed over 90 percent silver. The other, smaller disks were unmarked.

The silver bar weighing 35 pounds 8 1/2 ounces was stamped on the top surface in the upper left-hand quarter with the letters "UUCCCLVCEVALLUS" beside a larger "XC." Another unclear mark appeared below the stamp and there seemed to be no assayer's bite.

Most of the sixteen gold rings found on the site were very small, with simple geometric designs. Four were notable exceptions, however. The most elaborate of these contained a design around the outside of the ring, showing in sequence a cannon, a stack of cannon balls, a powder keg, a pike, a sword, a helmet and sword, a knight's plumed helmet with visor, a bugle, a drum and another cannon. Another ring was fashioned as a pair of hands holding a heart between the finger tips. Two others bore a crudely engraved floral design on a series of round facets, with six sharply pointed pyramids surrounding each ring like short spikes.

On the expanded handles of three of the five fragmentary forks found were three stamps: closest to the tines was the word "Gosalez" or "Gozalez" in a rectangle with the last three letters arranged below the first four. The middle stamp showed the Pillars of Hercules surmounted by a crown. Just below the crown and between the Pillars was an unidentified figure which seemed to be a knight's plumed helmet in outline. Below and between the bases of the pillars was a large letter "M." The stamp nearest the end of the handle was all but indiscernible.

The first stamp probably gave the family name of the manufacturers, or less likely, of an owner. The second stamp with crown and pillars when used on manufactured articles may have indicated that the piece was registered and assayed, but had not yet passed through the royal foundry, and that royal dues were still owed. The "M" was the symbol of the Mexico mint. The stamp containing two pillars, a crown and the letter "M" was found on the rim of one of the silver plates after it had been cleaned by electrolysis.

Not only was the large number of silver and gold coins found on the Colored Beach wreck valuable to numismatists, but the collection gave archaeologists an invaluable opportunity to learn about dies and minting practices of the early Spanish colonial period. Although the silver was generally damaged from salt-water corrosion, the gold coins were in excellent condition. The salvaged specimens represented a broad sample of Spanish colonial coins struck at all mints operating in the New World during the last of the reign of Charles II (1665-1700) and the first fifteen years of the reign of Philip V (1700-1724). Several factors contributed to making this a highly significant numismatic find. The gold coins were in a generally uncirculated condition and included denominations and types previously unknown or of which only a few examples were known to exist. This was true in the case of all the mints, but particularly for those at Bogotá, Colombia, and Cuzco, Peru. The majority of coins, however, was from the Mexico City mint.

Coins struck in New World mints during this period were usually irregularly shaped macuquinas or "cobs." The term "cob" comes from the Spanish cabo de barra, or "end of the bar," which described a step in the manufacture of the coins. Individual planchets (flat disks of metal ready for stamping as coins) were clipped in succession from the end of a strip of metal. After being trimmed to the proper weights, these irregular blanks were placed between two iron or steel dies into which designs for the coins had been impressed with a variety of puncheons. When forcibly struck, the dies were driven into the metal, producing the finished coins. Carelessness in the way they were struck, together with the fact that many times the planchets were smaller than the area covered by the engraving on the dies, caused most of the coins produced this way to show only part of the die design and seldom the date. The size and shape of the coins were evidently of little consequence. Supported by royal decree, an effort was made, however, to impress the mint mark and the assayer's initial on the coin. Silver, during this period, was minted in the New World in denominations of V2, 1, 2, 4, and 8 reals. Approximately 68 reals were struck from a mark of

248

silver weighing one-half pound. Gold, valued at 16 reals to one escudo, was minted in denominations of 1, 2,   4, and 8 escudos. The 8 escudo was also the doblon, equaling sixteen 8-real pieces or "pieces of eight." (For comparative purposes it may be noted that the real had an approximate value of 12 1/2 cents.)

Spanish colonial coinage at times has enjoyed great influence in other parts of the world, particularly in the Philippines and the Far East, but most importantly perhaps on the currency of the United States, whose first continental currency was made payable in Spanish 8-real pieces or milled dollars. The 2- and 4-real pieces became known as "two bits" and "four bits" respectively in the United States.

About 88 percent of the gold coins found on the Colored Beach Wreck were struck at the mint in Mexico City. Coining operations began there in 1536, although regular issues of gold coins did not begin until 1679. From its beginning, the mint operated as a more or less private enterprise until it was incorporated by decree into the royal treasury in 1732. Coins struck at this mint during the late 17th and early 18th centuries bore on the obverse face a shield showing the coats of arms of territories then under Spanish rule. To the right of the shield was the denomination of the coin, in Roman numerals for gold and in Arabic for silver. On the left were the mint mark and the assayer's initial. The legend around the coin read "Philippus V [or Carlos II] D.G. [date]."

The reverse of the coins usually showed a centered Jerusalem cross, enclosed in a tressure (bordering) design. Around the outside was a continuation of the legend from the obverse, "Hispaniarum et Indiarum Rex."

After 1700, when Charles II, a Hapsburg, died and Philip V of Anjou, a Bourbon, succeeded him, touching off the long, bitter War of the Spanish Succession, Mexico-mint coins reflected the change of monarchy. They are easily identified by the Bourbon shield of Philip V of Spain superimposed on a further modified Hapsburg shield. This remained unchanged until 1714, when the Bourbon device of three fleurs-de-lis was enlarged and other details of the design were made more harmonious.

Of the Mexico-mint coins in the state's 25 percent, about 45 percent, though undated, probably fell into the 1700-1713 period. Seven percent were dated between 1702 and 1713, but the concentration was in the years 1711-1713. This concentration very likely indicates when most of the undated coins were minted. Coins dated 1714 and 1715 made up slightly more than 45 percent of the Mexico-mint coins in the state's share. These dates probably reflect a lack of large fleet movements to Spain during the three to four years before1715 while the war was still in progress.

Of particular interest was a number of almost perfectly round gold coins struck in the Mexico mint. They were exceptions to the generally crude "cob" coins, and it was obvious that special care had been given to their production. The treasure hunters had found one 1695 8-escudo piece of Charles II, and seventeen others struck during the reign of Philip V—ten 8-escudo coins dated 1702, one 4-escudo coin dated 1713, one 1-escudo and five 8-escudo coins dated 1714. They were "Imperials," thought to have been the first strikes of particularly fine dies and intended as gifts for Spanish royalty. The 8-escudo piece was about the size of a silver dollar. The outer ring of lettering read, "Philippvs*V*Dei*G*1714 [Philip V, By the Grace of God, 1714]." To the left of the shield was the "M" surmounted by "o," signifying the Mexico City mint, and below this, the letter "J," evidently the mark of the assayer, Jose Eustaquio de Leon. To the right was the Roman numeral "VIII" telling the value, 8 escudos. The shield combined the coats of arms of Spain's provinces and possessions. Centered was the small shield and three fleurs-de-lis of the Bourbons. In the upper left corner of the larger shield, a castle tower symbolized Castile. To the right of this figure, a rampant lion represented Leon; other figures at the bottom represented the Low Countries, then the Spanish Netherlands. Vertical bars at the top right denoted Aragon; and to the right of them, long vertical bars with cross-beams stood for Naples and Sicily.

The mint at Lima, Peru, struck 1-, 2-, 4- and 8-escudo gold coins from the year 1696, in the reign of Charles II, and in that portion of the reign of Philip V covered by the collection. These coins consistently appeared to have been manufactured to higher standards than the coins of any other colonial mint of the time. The design of the coins, although quite different from that of the Mexico mint, did not change appreciably from the late 1690s through the first years of the reign of Philip V.

On the obverse the Lima coins bore the Jerusalem cross with the upper left and lower right quarters occupied by castles; the upper right and lower left quarters by lions inside circles of dots surrounded by the legend "Charles II [or Philip V], D.G. [By the Grace of God] Hispa [or Hisaniar]." The reverse carried the Pillars of Hercules rising from the sea in front of two horizontal lines. Above the top line in the left corner was the initial of the mint "L," between the columns the value of the coin in Arabic, and to the right the initial of the assayer. On the second line were the letters "P V A," the abbreviation for the motto "Plus Ultra," and the last three digits of the date just above the waves of the sea. Over the Pillars was a crown from the sides of which extended a series of circular dots enclosing all of the above symbols. The legend around the dots read, "Et Indiarum Rex," a continuation of that from the obverse, also enclosed in a dotted circle. In some issues the legend began on the reverse and ended on the obverse face of the coin. The 1-escudo coins also varied, with a single castle and the mint initial on the left, the assayer's initial on the right, and the last three numbers of the date below.

The Santa Fe Bogotá mint in Colombia may have been the first in the New World to coin gold regularly, but there is little positive information available on its minting practices until well into the 18th century. The Colored Beach Wreck yielded 1- and 2-escudo pieces. Previously, rare-coin experts had recorded only one 2-escudo piece of Charles II, and the earliest 1-escudo piece was given as 1736.

These coins were generally crude and irregular. The Spanish arms were incomplete on many specimens, and the coats of arms of the various countries were often incorrectly portrayed. One of the most frequent errors was the reversal in positions of the castles and lions in the arms of Leon and Castile. Occasionally, the entire field was reversed, with Leon and Castile appearing on the right and the cross of the Kingdoms of Naples and Sicily on the left. Lack of consistency in the coins, compounded by poor workmanship, made it difficult to determine their dates of manufacture. Quite possibly the use of unskilled native labor at the mint was responsible for the crude character of the coins.

The mint at Cuzco, Peru, apparently operated for only a few months in 1698. Essentially, coins were like those from Lima with the exception of the mint mark, which was in this case a "C." Previously, only one 2-escudo coin from 1698 was known to exist.

At least ten examples were recovered from the wreck site: a 1-escudo and nine 2-escudo coins. The 1-escudo piece resembled that of Lima, with a single small castle flanked on the left by the mint mark and on the right by the assayer's initial. Underneath were the last three digits of the date.

The division between the state and the salvagers of the 200-odd pounds of silver coins by weight made it impossible for Clausen to learn much about mints, denominations and dates of these coins. His general observations and examination of them, however, indicated that the majority were of Mexican origin dating from 1700 to 1714. A small percentage were from the Lima mint, some from the late 1600s, with an even smaller proportion from the mint at Potosi in present-day Bolivia. Although all three of these mints were striking full series of denominations in silver —1/2, 1, 2, 4, and 8 reals—between 1700 and 1714, most of the coins found were 4 and 8 reals.

Despite the lack of variety in common artifacts, those in the treasure category were unsurpassed. The recovered specimens provided first-hand evidence of what actually comprised treasure moving from the New World to Spain during this period. From the large number of Mexican-minted coins in the find, it appears that the wreck was one of the five vessels of the Flat a under the command of Esteban de Ubilla which loaded at Vera Cruz. The size and number of cannon found indicated that it was probably one of the smaller vessels, possibly a patache, and since the vessel had been badly broken up and its contents widely scattered, the early Spanish salvagers had missed getting this treasure.

Bibliography

Anderson, Romola and R. C., The Sailing-Ship, Six Thousand
Years of History, W. W. Norton and Co., New York, 1963.

Atwater, James, "Spanish Gold Two Fathoms Deep," Saturday
Evening Post, December 12, 1964.

Ault, Warren O., Europe in Modem Times, D. C. Heath and
Company, Boston, 1946.

Burgess, Robert F., Sinkings, Salvages and Shipwrecks,
American Heritage Press, New York, 1970.

Clausen, Carl J., "The Proton Magnetometer: Its Use in
Plotting the Ferrous Components of a Shipwreck Site as
an Aid to Archaeological Interpretations," The Florida
Anthropologist, Vol. XIX, Nos. 2-3, June-September, 1966.

Clausen, Carl J., "A 1715 Spanish Treasure Ship,"
Contributions of the Florida State Museum, Social
Sciences, No. 12, University of Florida, Gainesville, 1965.

Coffman, F. L., 1001 Lost, Buried or Sunken Treasures,
Thomas Nelson & Company, New York, 1957.

Covington, James W., Pirates, Indians, and Spaniards, Father
Escobedo's "La Florida," Greater Outdoors Publishing
Company, St. Petersburg, Florida, 1963.

Dana, Richard Henry, Two Years Before the Mast, Harper and
Brothers, New York, 1846.

Defant, Albert, Volume II of Physical Oceanography, The
Macmillan Company, New York, 1961.

Dickinson, Jonathan, God's Protecting Providence, Being the
Narrative of a Journey from Port Royal in Jamaica to
Philadelphia between August 23,1696, and April 1, 1697
(E. W. and C. M. Andrews, eds.), Yale University Press,
New Haven, 1961.

Editors of the American Heritage, The American Heritage

History of the Thirteen Colonies, American Heritage
Publishing Company, New York, 1967.

Esquemeling, John, The Buccaneers of America, George Allen
& Unwin Limited, London, 1951.

Fernandez Duro, Cesareo, Armada Espanola, Vol. 6, Madrid,
1900.

Goggin, John M., Indian and Spanish Selected Writings,
University of Miami Press, Miami, 1964.

Higgs, Charles D., "Spanish Contacts with the Ais (Indian
River) Country," Florida Historical Quarterly, Vol. 21,
1942.

Lever, Darcy, The Young Sea Officer's Sheet Anchor, Edward
W. Sweetman Company, New York, 1963.

Luce, S. B., Text-Book of Seamanship, Cornell Maritime Press,
Cambridge, Maryland, 1950.

MacLiesh, Fleming, and Krieger, Martin L., The Privateers,
Random House, New York, 1962.

Manucy, Albert, The Houses of St. Augustine 1565-1821, The
St. Augustine Historical Society, St. Augustine, Florida,
1962.

Marx, Robert F., Shipwrecks in Florida Waters, Scott
Publishing Company, Eau Gallie, Florida, 1969.

Marx, Robert F., 77ie Treasure Fleets of the Spanish Main, The
World Publishing Company, Cleveland and New York,
1968.

Nesmith, Robert I., Dig for Pirate Treasure, The Devin-Adair
Company, New York, 1959.

Parry, J. H., The Age of Reconnaissance, The New American
Library, New York, 1963.

Plenderleith, H. J., The Conservation of Antiquities and Works
of Art, Oxford University Press, New York and Oxford,
1962.

Potter, John S., Jr., The Treasure Diver's Guide, Doubleday &
Co., New York, 1960.

Romans, Bernard, A Concise Natural History of East and West
Florida, A Facsimile Reproduction of the 1775 Edition,

University of Florida Press, Gainesville, 1962.

Rouse, Irving, A Survey of Indian River Archaeology, Yale University Press, New Haven, 1951.

Schurz, William Lytle, The Manila Galleon, E. P. Dutton and Company, New York, 1939.

Shepard, Francis P., Submarine Geology, 2d ed. Harper & Row, New York, 1963.

Ships, Paul Hamlyn Limited, London, 1963.

Smith, Hale G., "Two Archaeological Sites in Brevard County, Florida," Florida Anthropological Society Publications, Number 1, University of Florida, Gainesville, 1949.

Steel's Elements of Mastmaking, Sailmaking and Rigging (from the 1794 edition), Edward W. Sweetman Company, New York, 1932.

Tooley, R. V., Maps and Mapmakers, Bonanza Books, Great Britain, 1962.

Villiers, Captain Alan, and others. Men, Ships and the Sea, National Geographic Society, Washington, D.C., 1962.

Wagner, Kip, "Drowned Galleons Yield Spanish Gold," National Geographic Magazine, January, 1965.

Wagner, Kip, and Taylor, L. B., Jr., Pieces of Eight, E. P. Dutton and Company, New York, 1966.

Whipple, A. B. C., Pirate; Rascals of the Spanish Main, Doubleday and Company, New York, 1957.

Worcester, Donald E., and Schaeffer, Wendell G,, The Growth and Culture of Latin America, Oxford University Press, New York and Oxford, 1956.

For more books about shipwrecks, diving, and treasure please see the publications of Robert F. Burgess at: **http://www.amazon.com/author/robert-f-burgess**

Made in United States
Troutdale, OR
08/27/2024